CURSIVE HANDWRITING WORKBOOK FOR TEENS

WHAT YOU WILL LEARN FROM THIS BOOK

This workbook is divided into the following parts.

Part 1: The Alphabet
Use the dot-to-dot method to learn how to correctly form every letter of the alphabet - both uppercase and lowercase.

Connecting Letters
Learn how to correctly join letters together so you can move on to writing words and sentences.

Part 2: Writing Words
Practice writing a specially chosen selection of words. The words increase in complexity as you work through this section.

Part 3: Writing Sentences
Now you practice writing full sentences using all of the skills you have learnt so far. By the end of this section you will be confidently writing in cursive.

Copyright © 2020

All rights reserved. No part of this publication may be reproduced, distributed, or transmitted in any form or by any means, including photocopying, recording, or other electronic or mechanical methods, without the prior written permission of the publisher, except in the case of brief quotations embodied in critical reviews and certain other noncommercial uses permitted by copyright law. For permission requests, contact the publisher.

Part 1: Cursive Alphabet

a b c d e f g h i j k l m n o p q r s t u v w x y z

Starting at number 1, trace the letter by following the order of numbered circles.

Trace the letters using the example above.

a a a a a a a a a a

a a a a a a a a a a

a a a a a a a a a a

Now write the letter on your own.

a

aBCDEFGHIJKLMNOPQRSTUVWXYZ

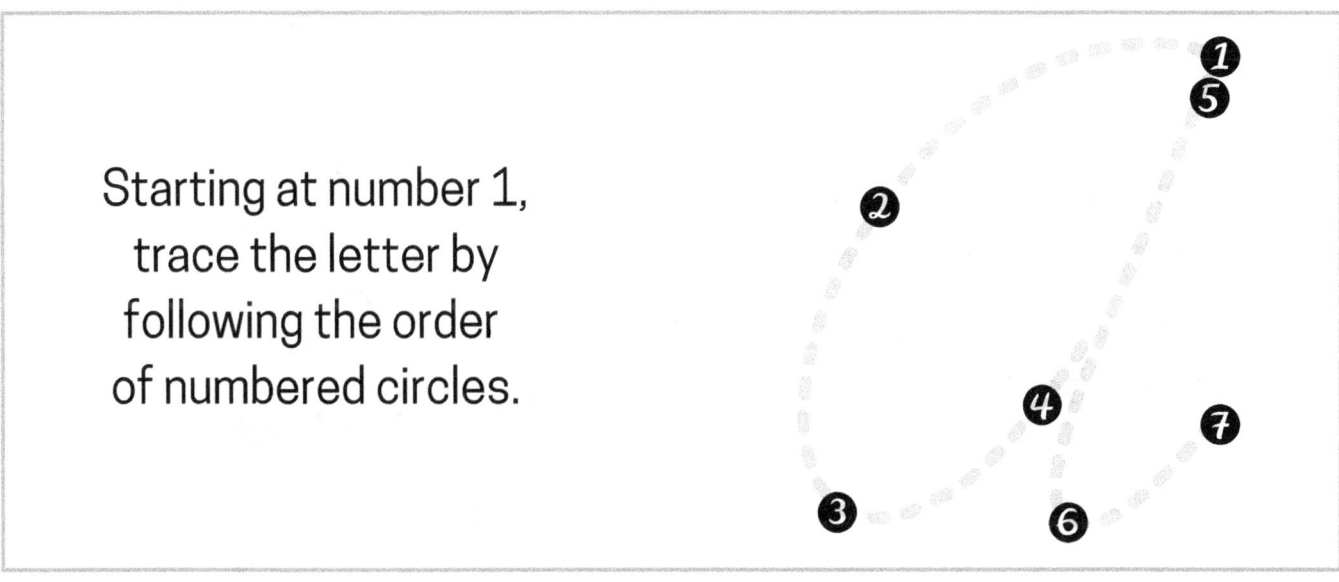

Starting at number 1, trace the letter by following the order of numbered circles.

Trace the letters using the example above.

a a a a a a a

a a a a a a a

a a a a a a a

Now write the letter on your own.

a

a **b** c d e f g h i j k l m n o p q r s t u v w x y z

Starting at number 1, trace the letter by following the order of numbered circles.

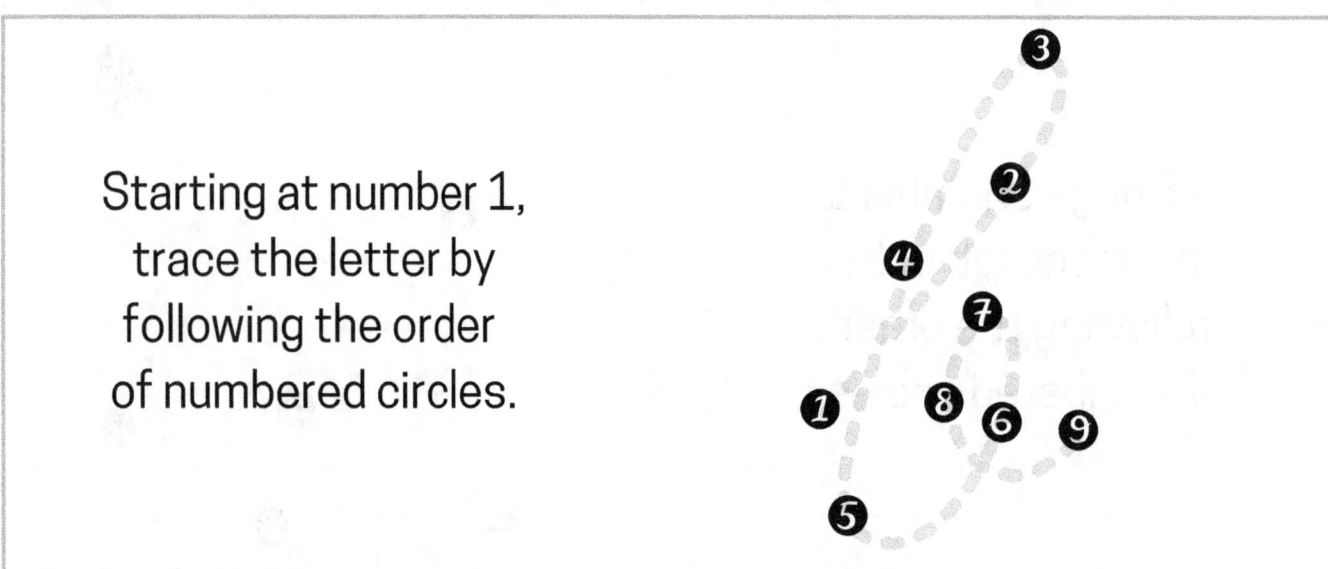

Trace the letters using the example above.

b b b b b b b b b b b

b b b b b b b b b b b

b b b b b b b b b b b

Now write the letter on your own.

b

a B C D E F G H I J K L M N O P Q R S T U V W X Y Z

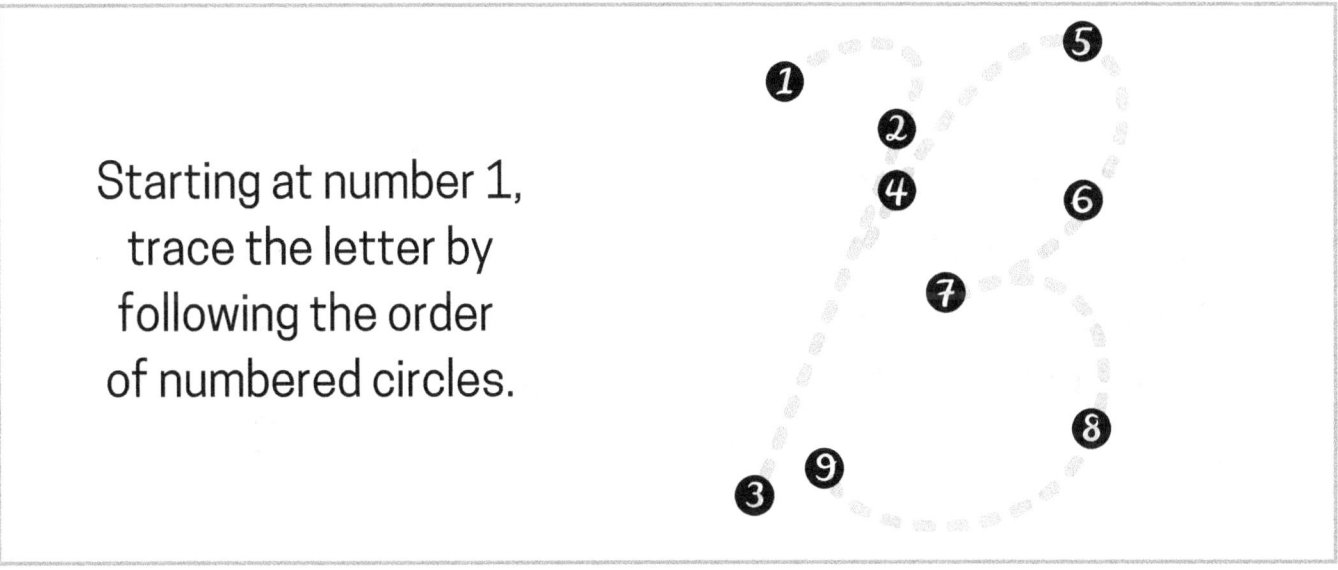

Starting at number 1, trace the letter by following the order of numbered circles.

Trace the letters using the example above.

Now write the letter on your own.

a b **c** d e f g h i j k l m n o p q r s t u v w x y z

Starting at number 1, trace the letter by following the order of numbered circles.

Trace the letters using the example above.

c c c c c c c c c c c

c c c c c c c c c c c

c c c c c c c c c c c

Now write the letter on your own.

c

a B **C** D E F G H I J K L M N O P Q R S T U V W X Y Z

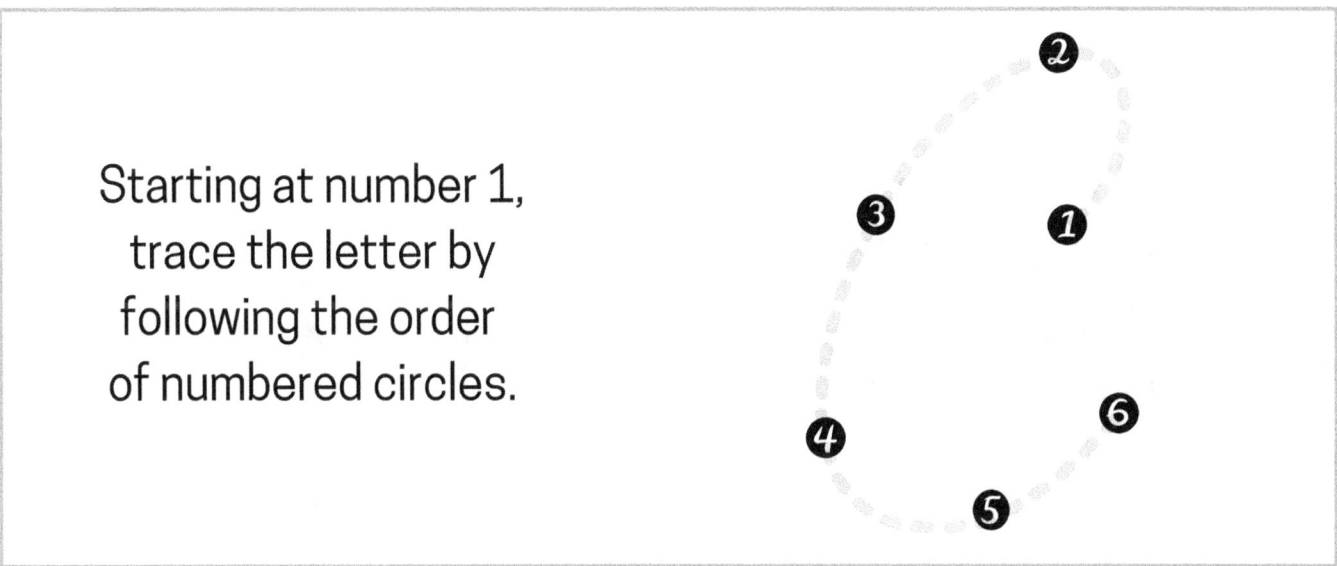

Starting at number 1, trace the letter by following the order of numbered circles.

Trace the letters using the example above.

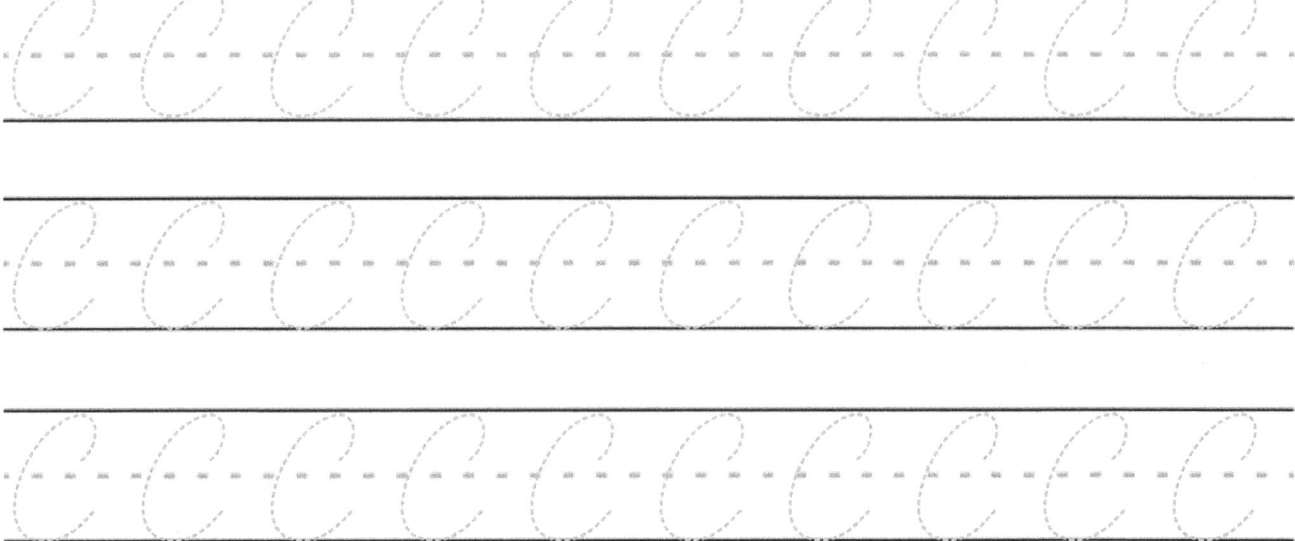

Now write the letter on your own.

C

a b c **d** e f g h i j k l m n o p q r s t u v w x y z

Starting at number 1, trace the letter by following the order of numbered circles.

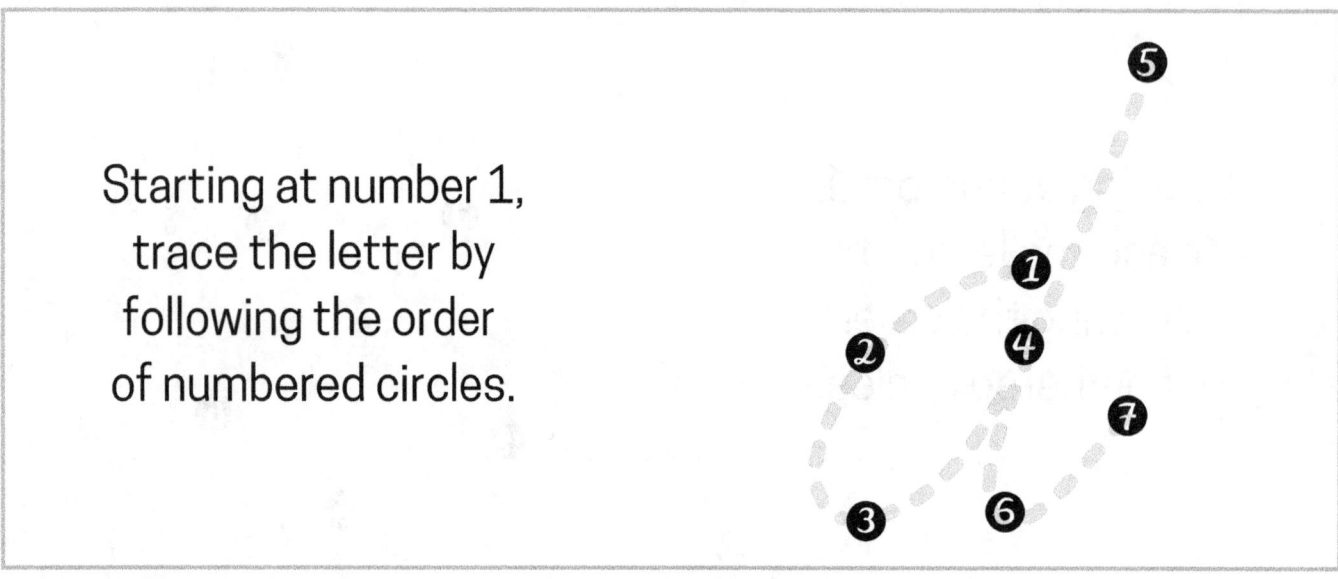

Trace the letters using the example above.

d d d d d d d d d

d d d d d d d d d

d d d d d d d d d

Now write the letter on your own.

d

a B C **D** *E F G H I J K L M N O P Q R S T U V W X Y Z*

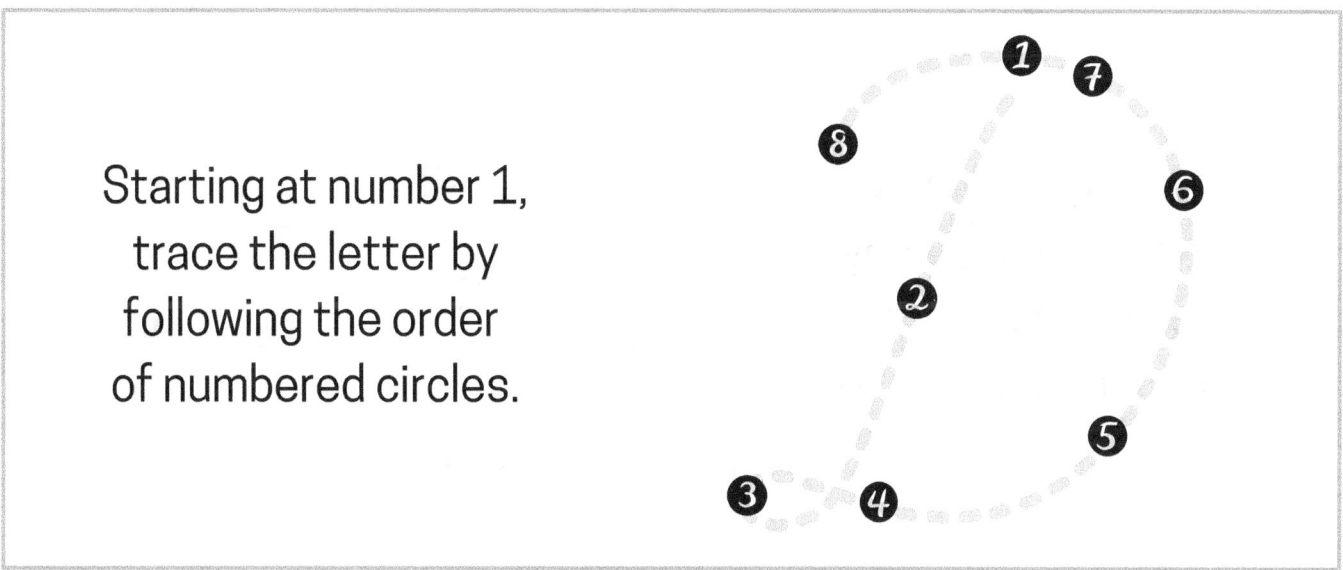

Starting at number 1, trace the letter by following the order of numbered circles.

Trace the letters using the example above.

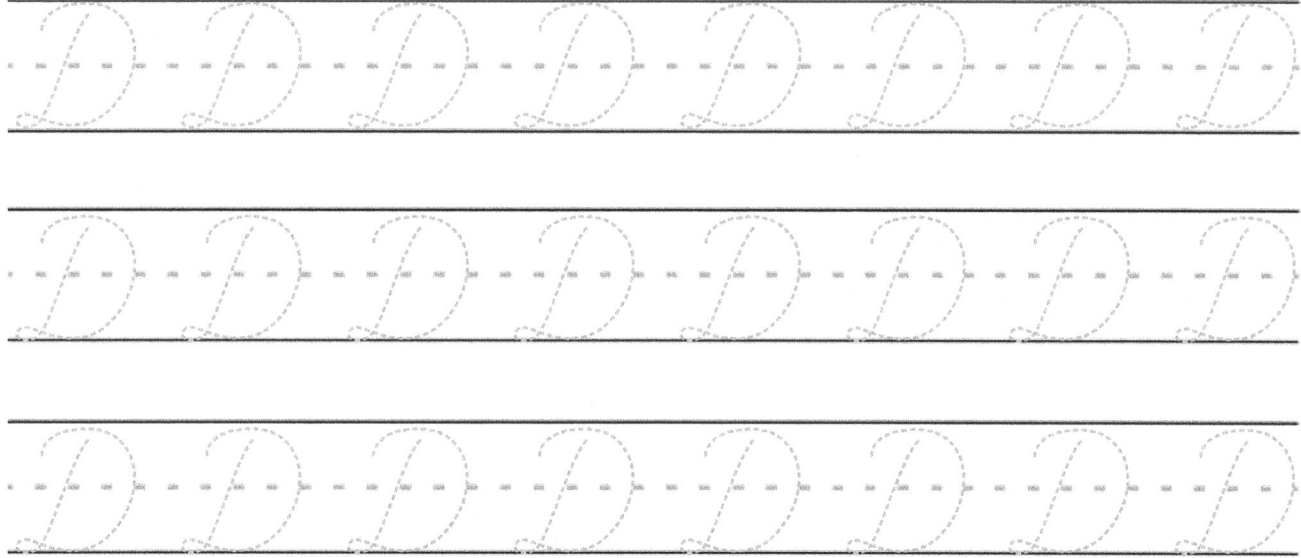

Now write the letter on your own.

a b c d **e** f g h i j k l m n o p q r s t u v w x y z

Starting at number 1, trace the letter by following the order of numbered circles.

Trace the letters using the example above.

e e e e e e e e e e e e e

e e e e e e e e e e e e e

e e e e e e e e e e e e e

Now write the letter on your own.

e

A B C D **E** *F G H I J K L M N O P Q R S T U V W X Y Z*

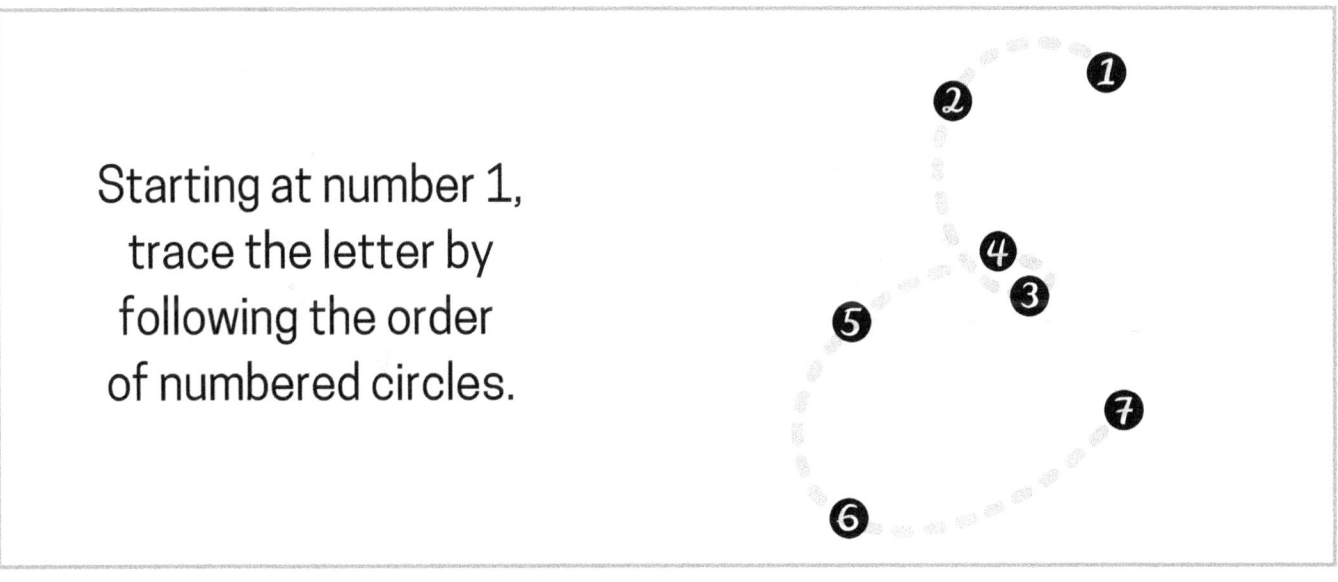

Starting at number 1, trace the letter by following the order of numbered circles.

Trace the letters using the example above.

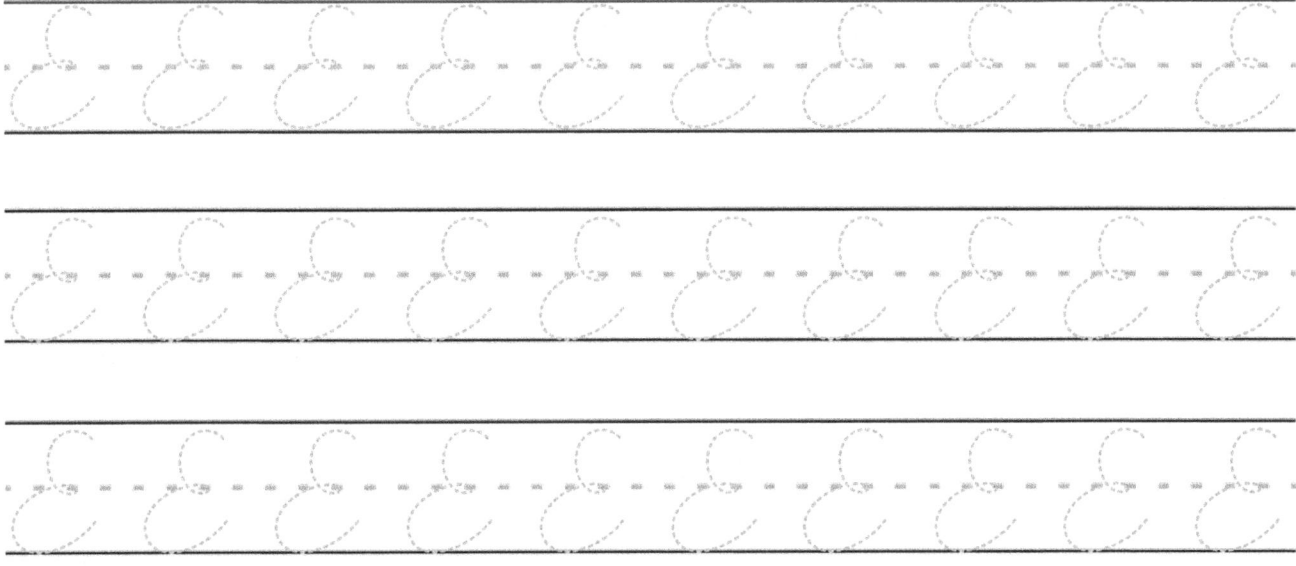

Now write the letter on your own.

*a b c d e **f** g h i j k l m n o p q r s t u v w x y z*

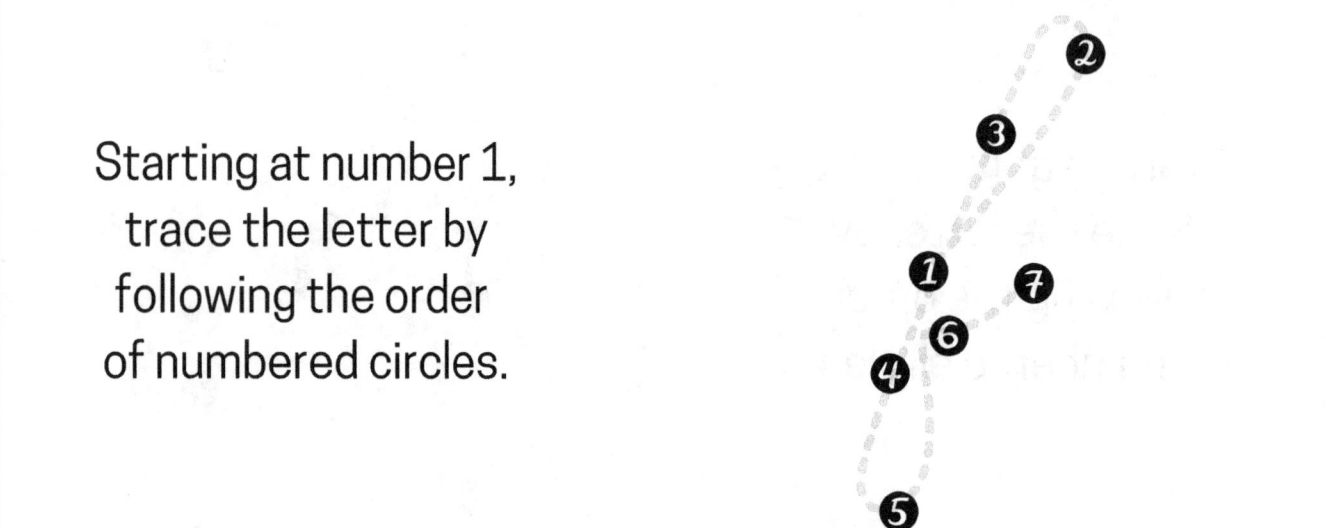

Starting at number 1, trace the letter by following the order of numbered circles.

Trace the letters using the example above.

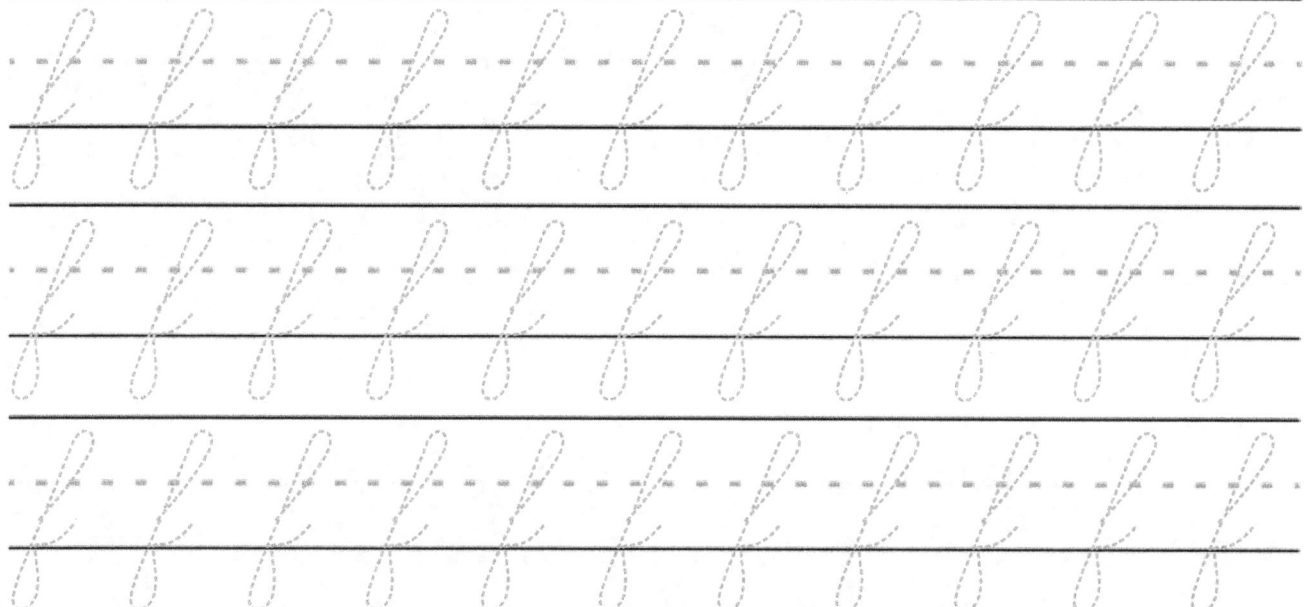

Now write the letter on your own.

A B C D E **F** *G H I J K L M N O P Q R S T U V W X Y Z*

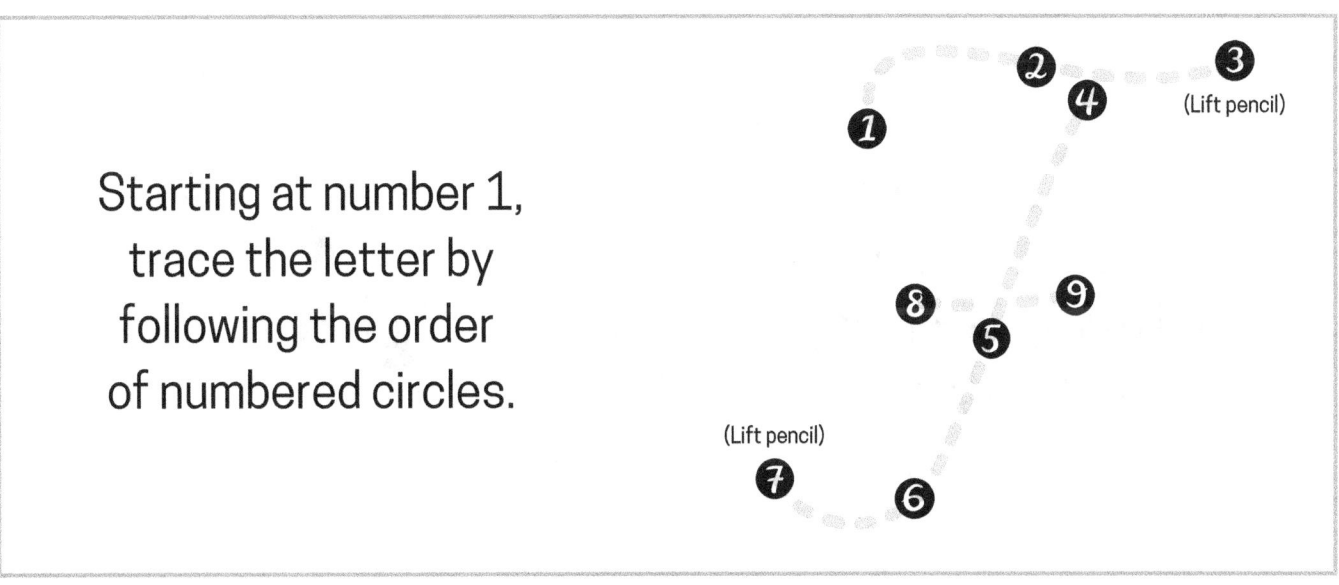

Starting at number 1, trace the letter by following the order of numbered circles.

Trace the letters using the example above.

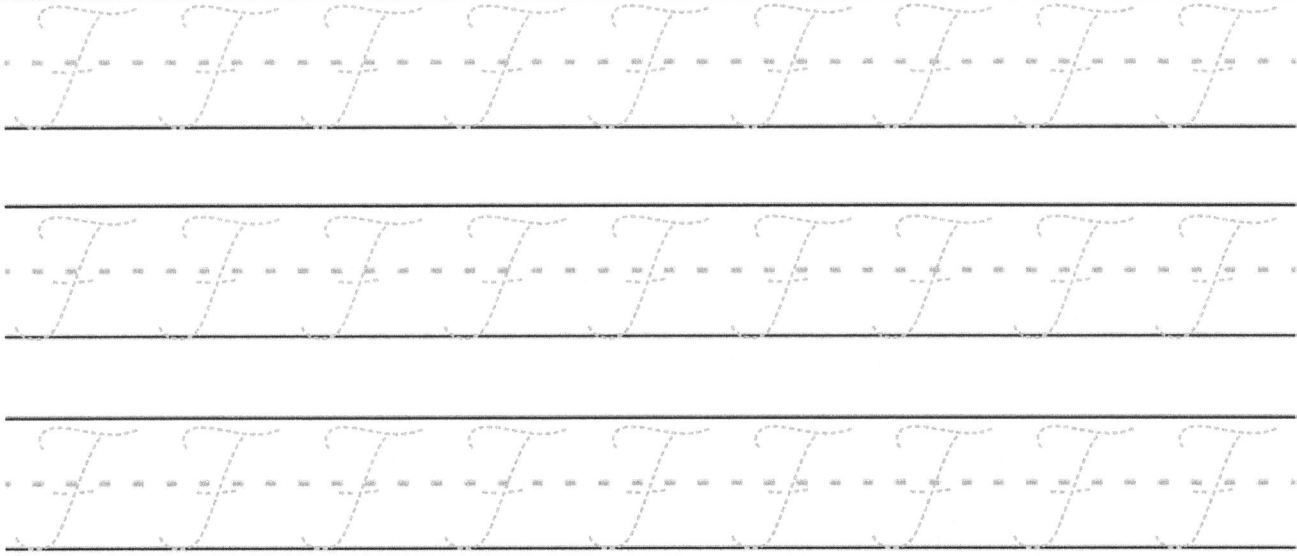

Now write the letter on your own.

F

a b c d e f **g** h i j k l m n o p q r s t u v w x y z

Starting at number 1, trace the letter by following the order of numbered circles.

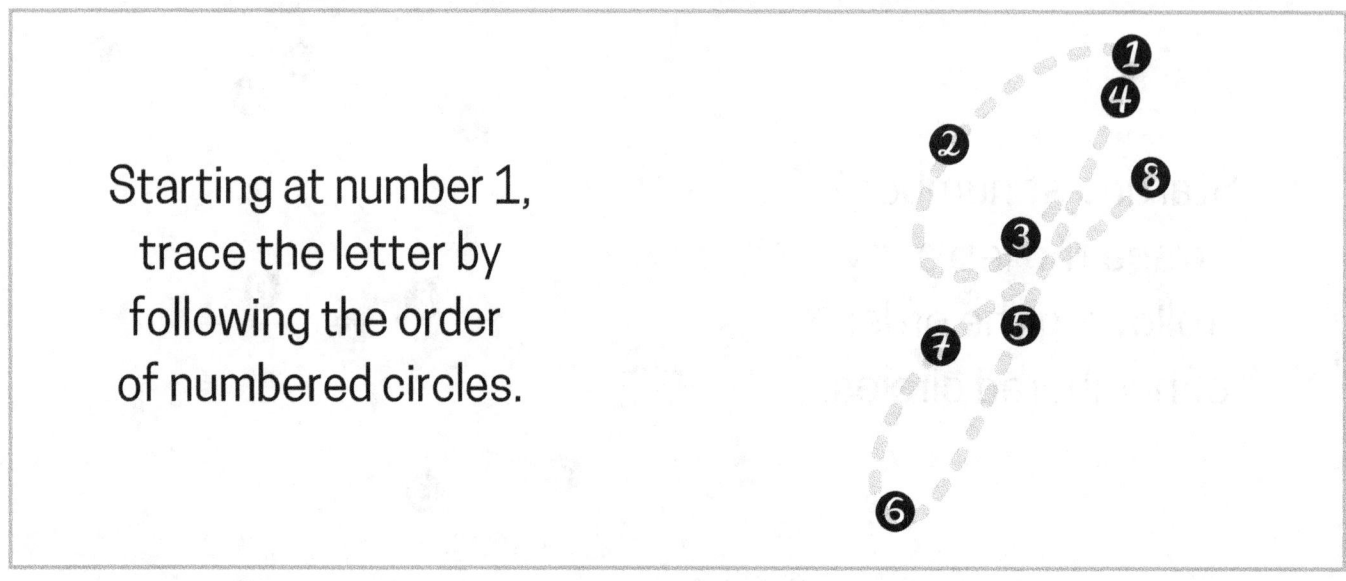

Trace the letters using the example above.

Now write the letter on your own.

*A B C D E F **G** H I J K L M N O P Q R S T U V W X Y Z*

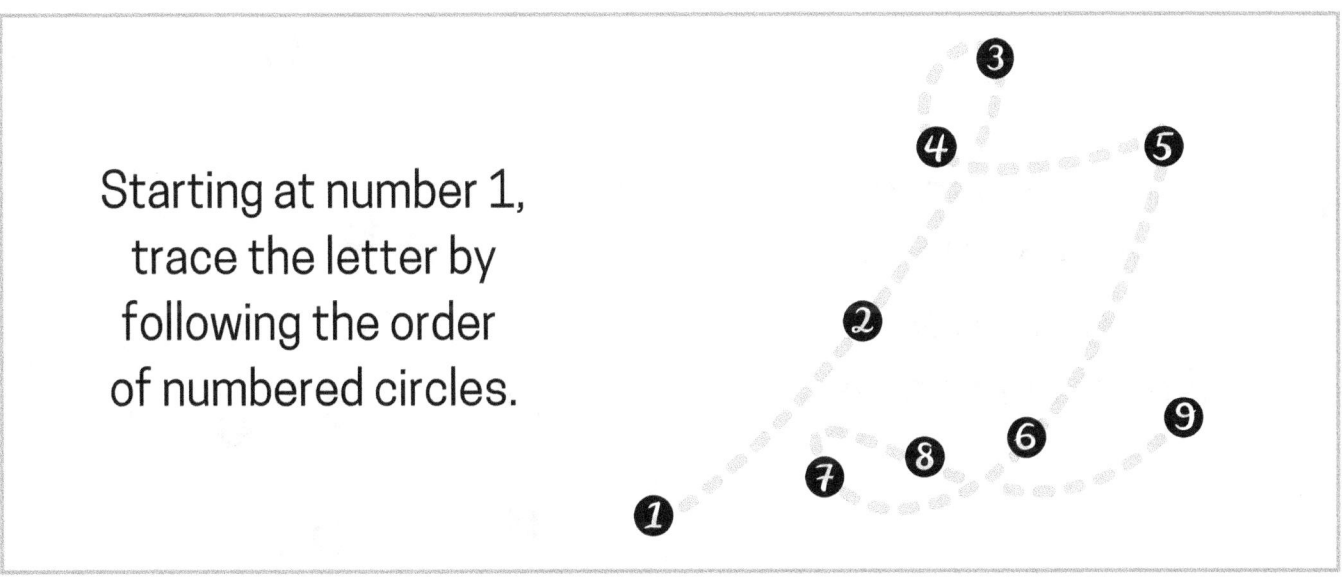

Starting at number 1, trace the letter by following the order of numbered circles.

Trace the letters using the example above.

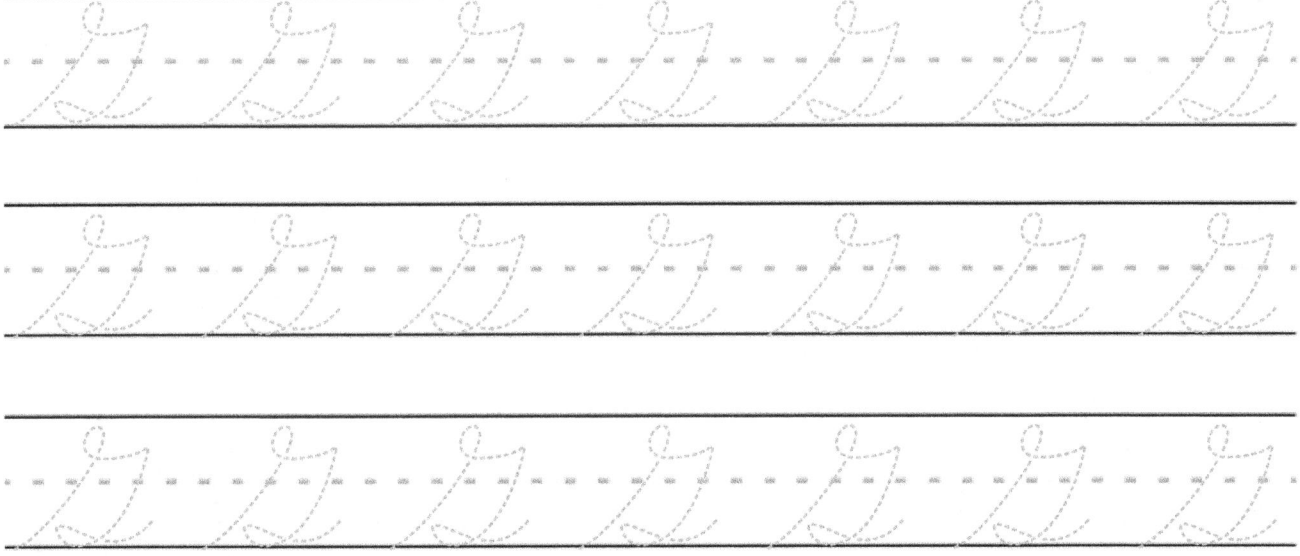

Now write the letter on your own.

a b c d e f g **h** i j k l m n o p q r s t u v w x y z

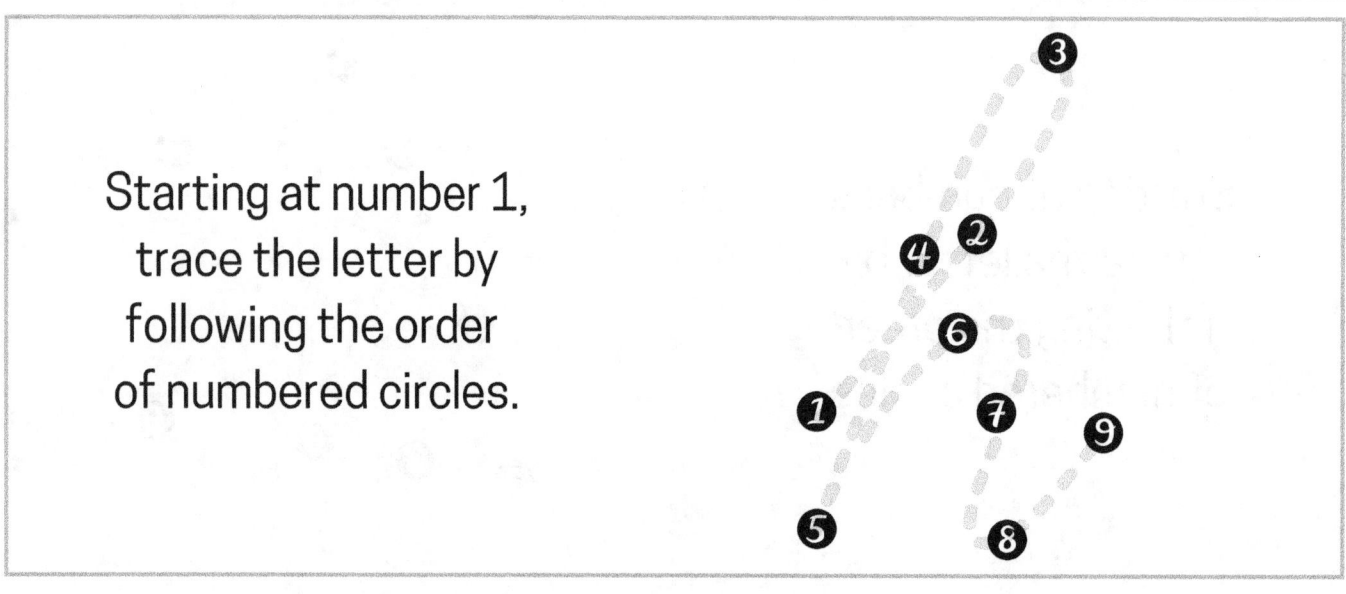

Starting at number 1, trace the letter by following the order of numbered circles.

Trace the letters using the example above.

h h h h h h h h h

h h h h h h h h h

h h h h h h h h h

Now write the letter on your own.

h

*A B C D E F G **H** I J K L M N O P Q R S T U V W X Y Z*

Starting at number 1, trace the letter by following the order of numbered circles.

① ④
②
⑧ ⑨
⑤
⑦ (Lift pencil)
③ (Lift pencil) ⑥

Trace the letters using the example above.

Now write the letter on your own.

H

a b c d e f g h **i** j k l m n o p q r s t u v w x y z

Starting at number 1, trace the letter by following the order of numbered circles.

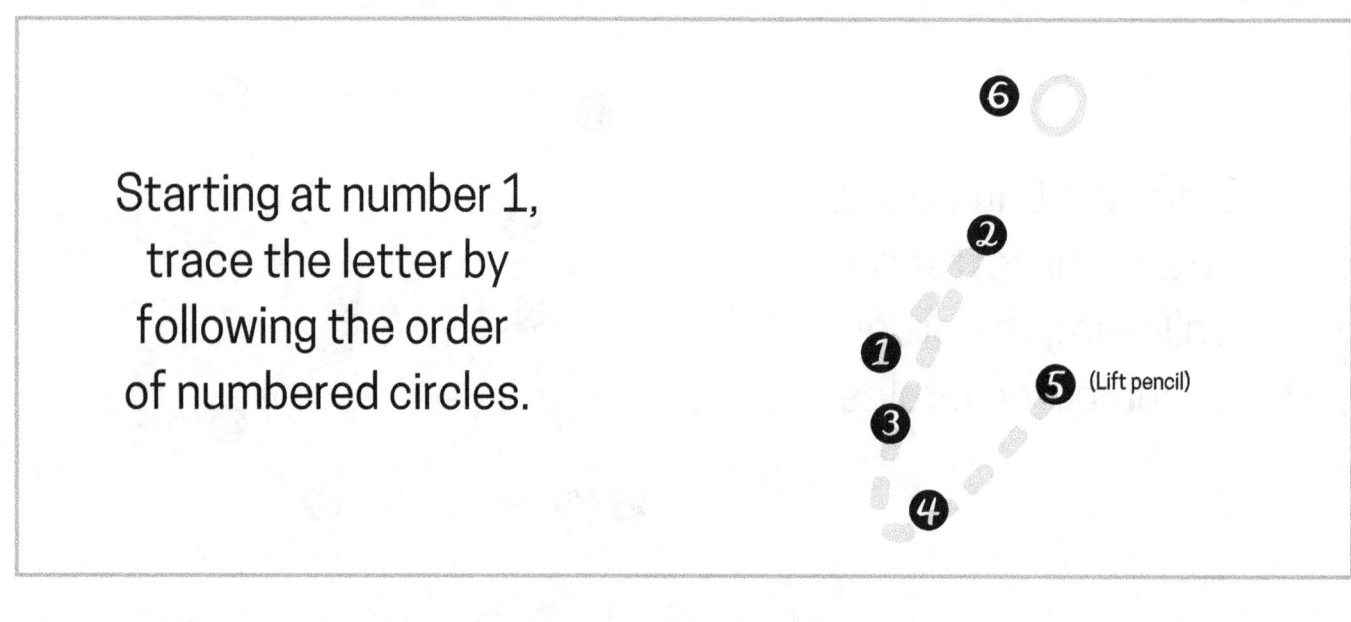

Trace the letters using the example above.

Now write the letter on your own.

i

A B C D E F G H I J K L M N O P Q R S T U V W X Y Z

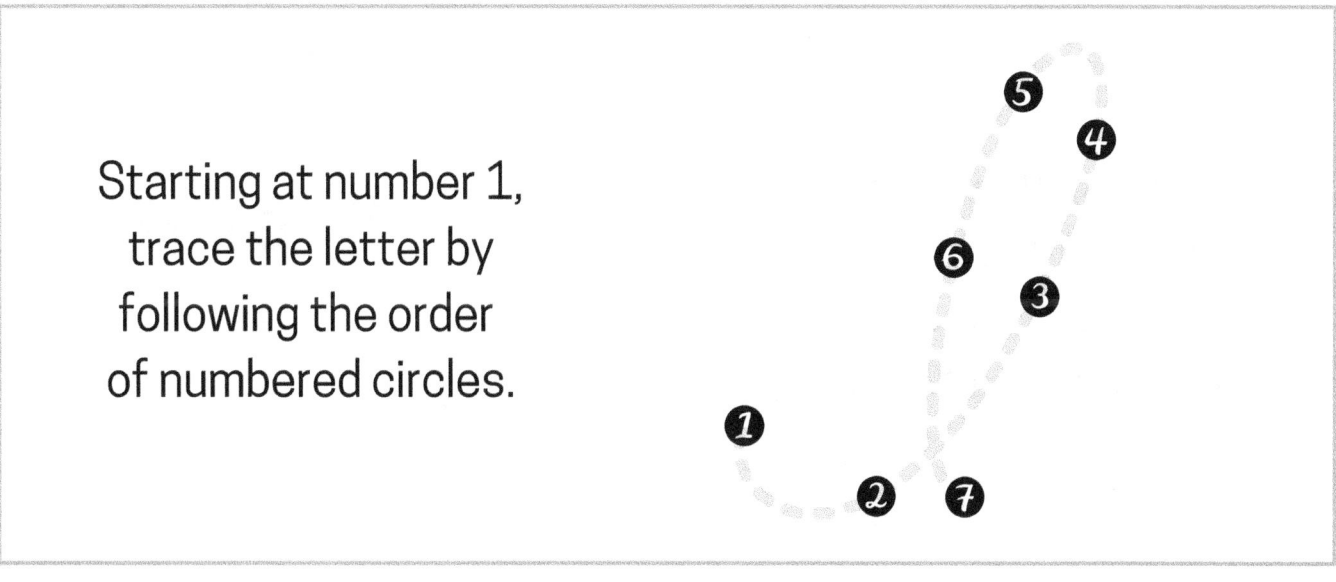

Starting at number 1, trace the letter by following the order of numbered circles.

Trace the letters using the example above.

Now write the letter on your own.

a b c d e f g h i **j** k l m n o p q r s t u v w x y z

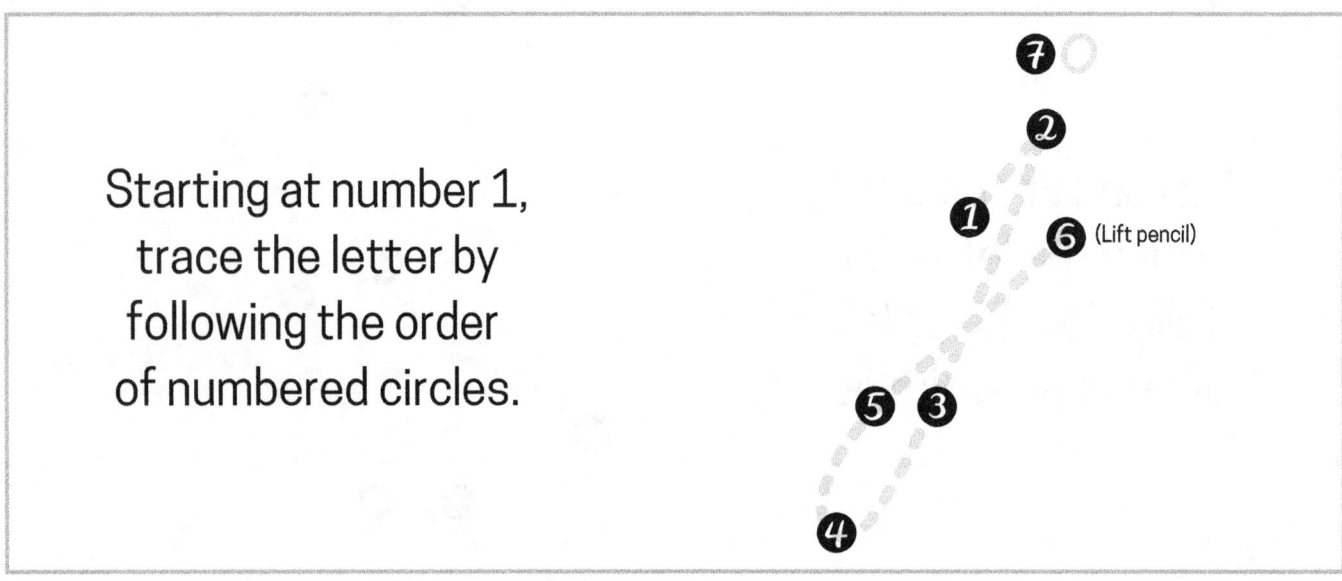

Starting at number 1, trace the letter by following the order of numbered circles.

Trace the letters using the example above.

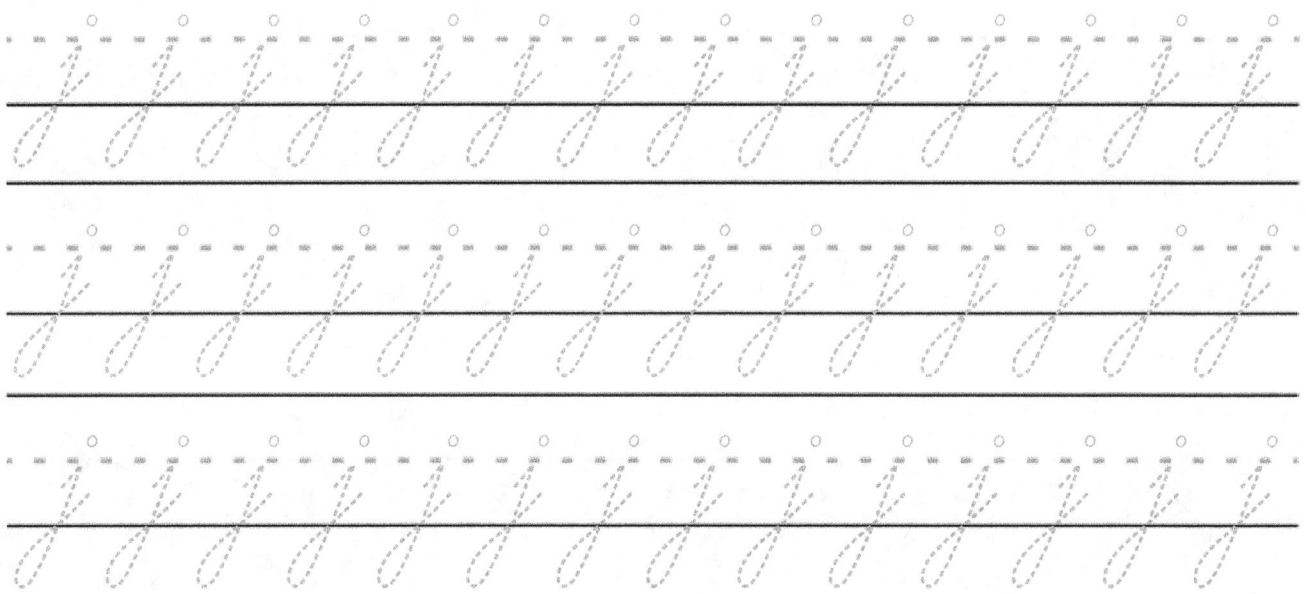

Now write the letter on your own.

j

*A B C D E F G H I **J** K L M N O P Q R S T U V W X Y Z*

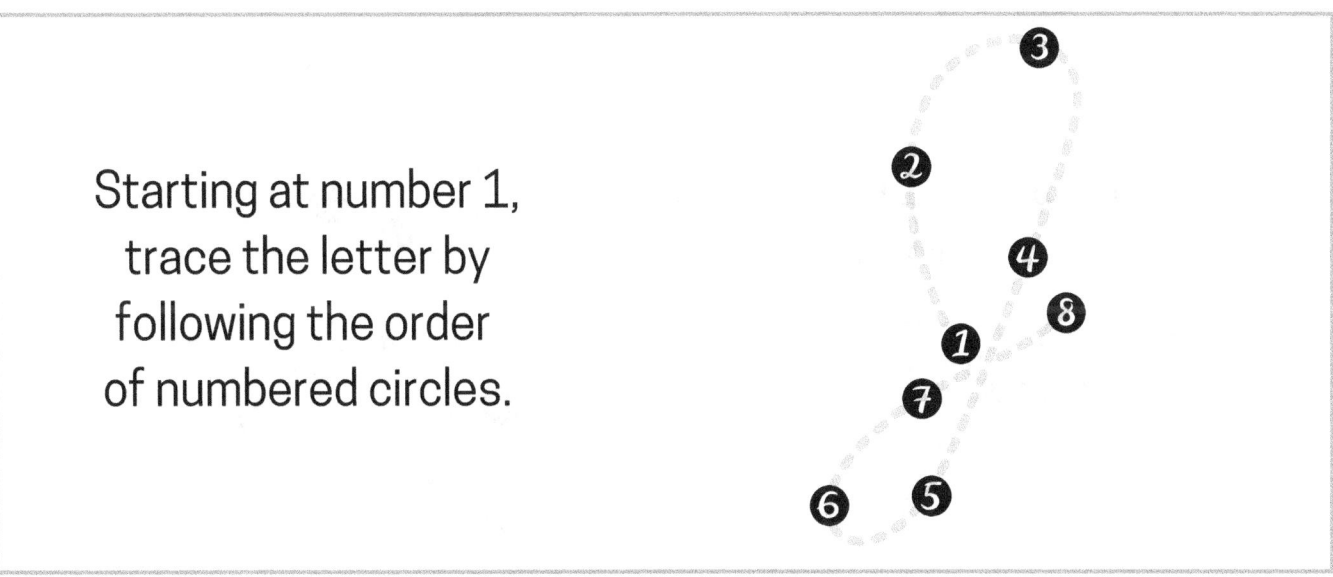

Starting at number 1, trace the letter by following the order of numbered circles.

Trace the letters using the example above.

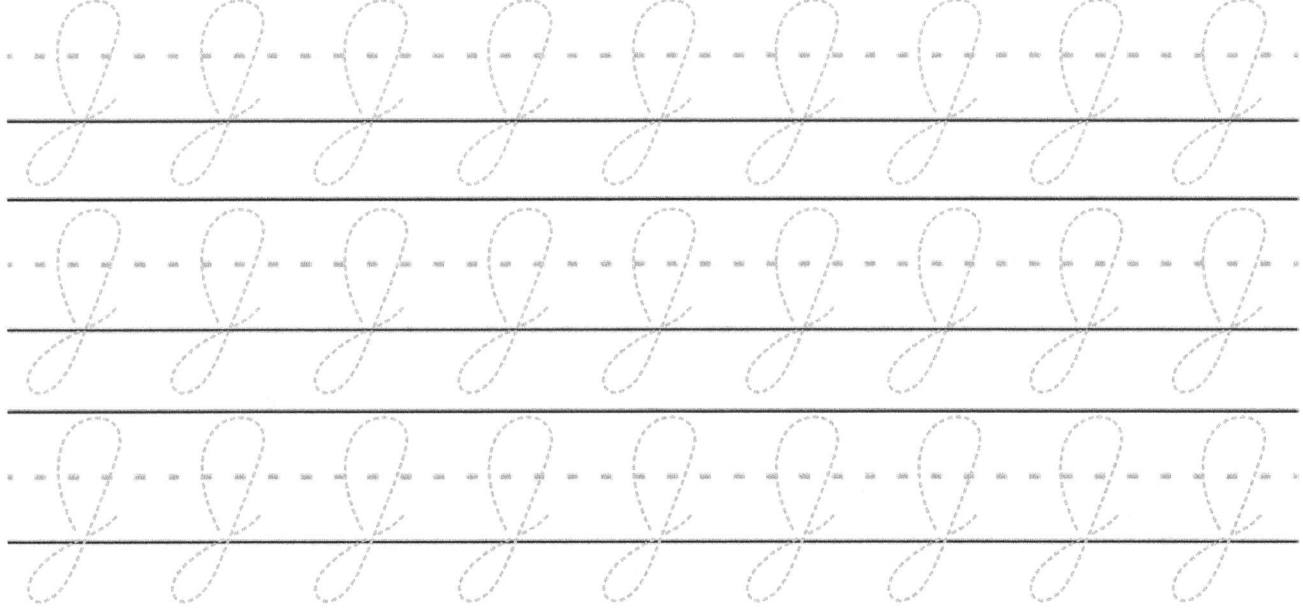

Now write the letter on your own.

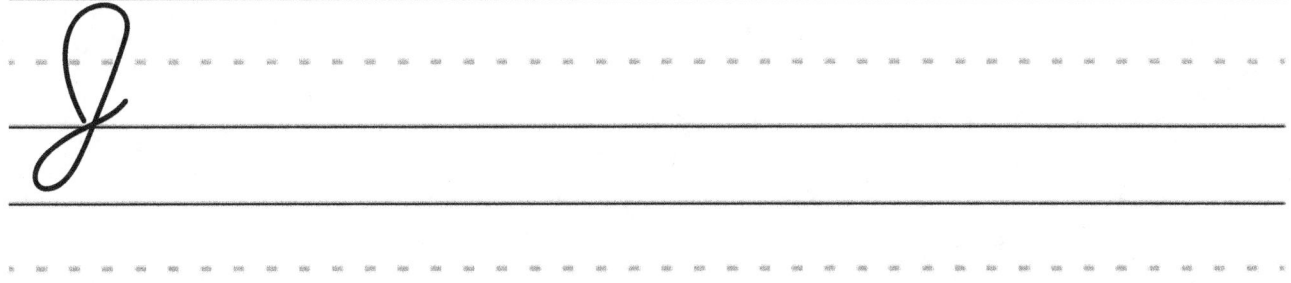

a b c d e f g h i j **k** l m n o p q r s t u v w x y z

Starting at number 1, trace the letter by following the order of numbered circles.

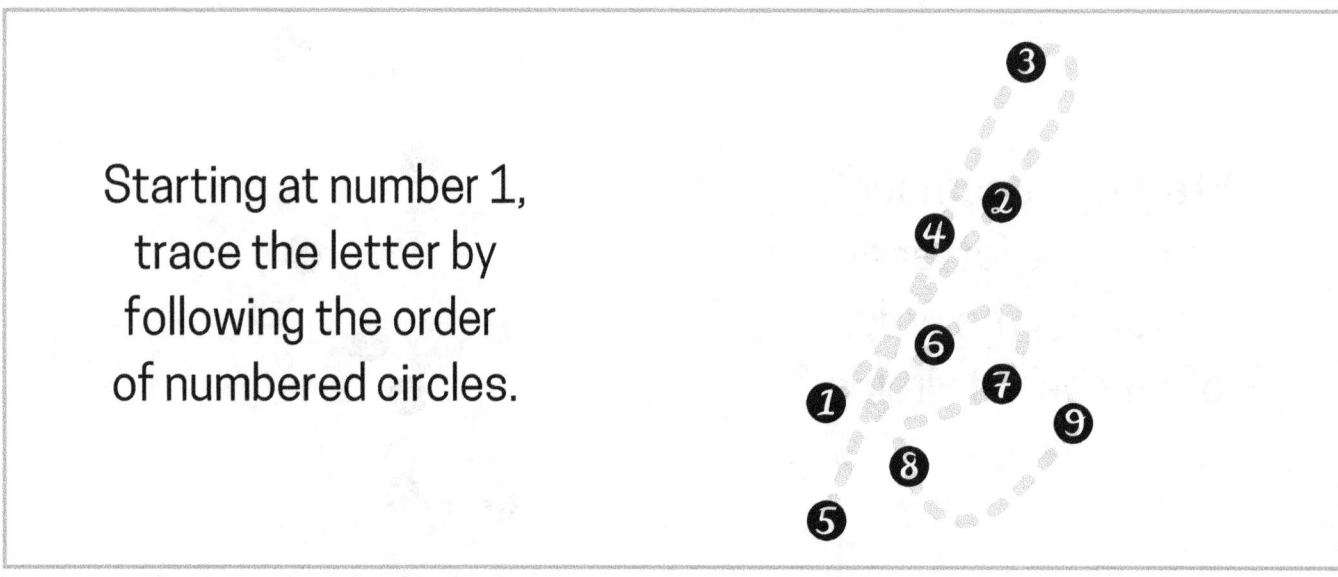

Trace the letters using the example above.

Now write the letter on your own.

a B C D E F G H I J **K** L M N O P Q R S T U V W X Y Z

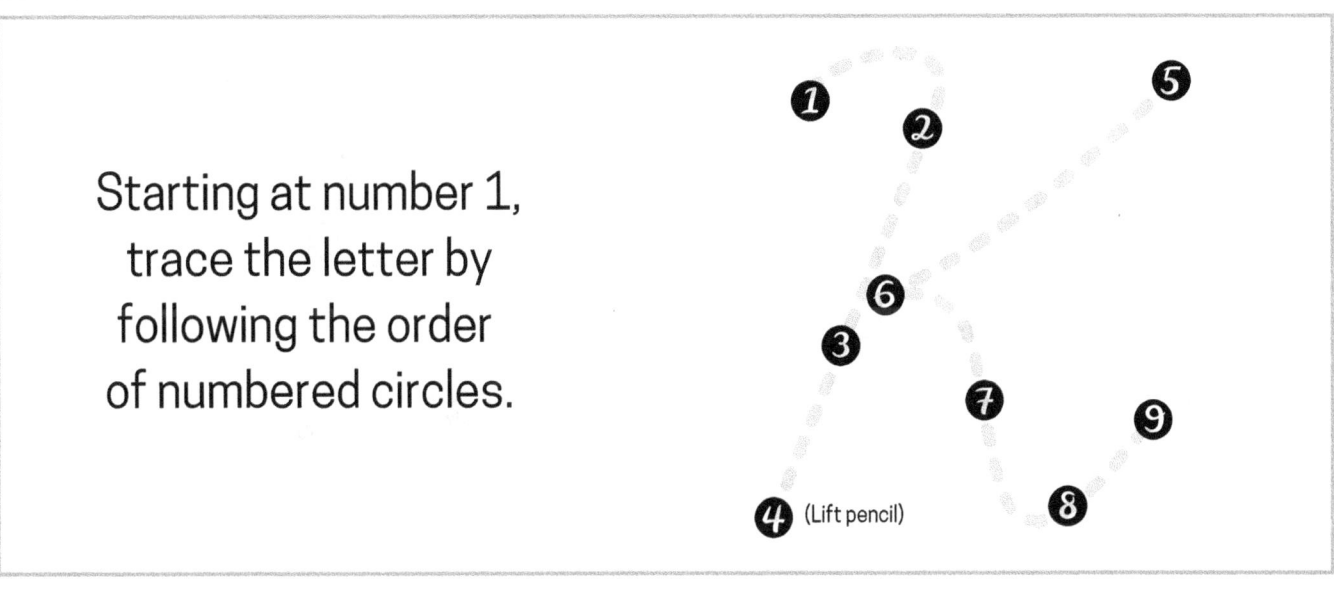

Starting at number 1, trace the letter by following the order of numbered circles.

Trace the letters using the example above.

Now write the letter on your own.

K

a b c d e f g h i j k **l** m n o p q r s t u v w x y z

Starting at number 1, trace the letter by following the order of numbered circles.

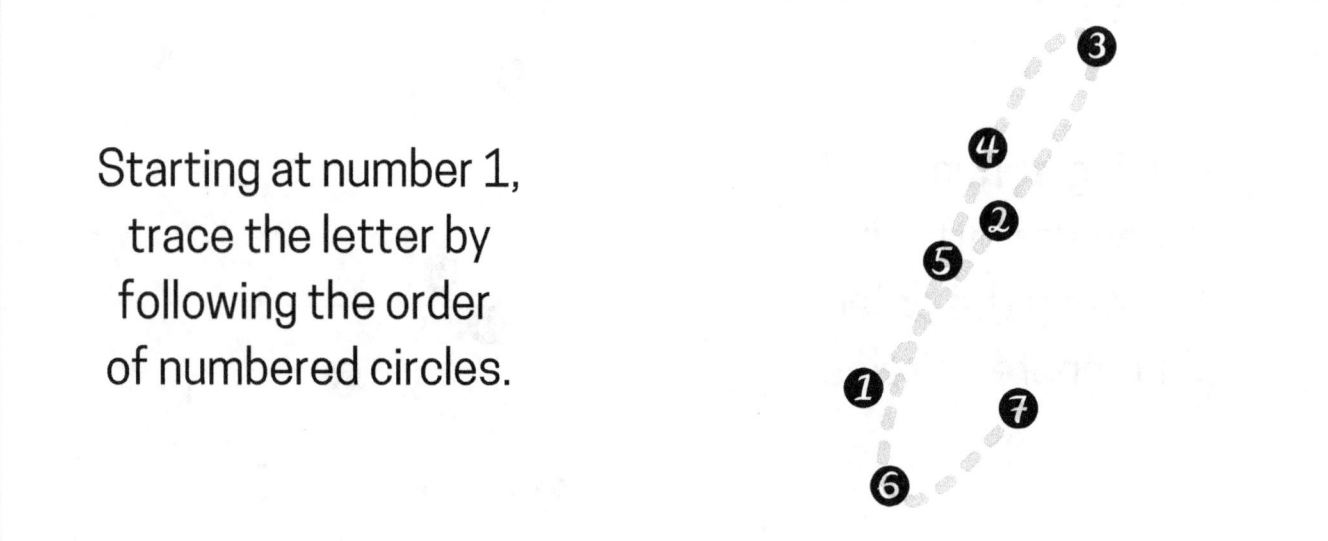

Trace the letters using the example above.

𝓁 𝓁 𝓁 𝓁 𝓁 𝓁 𝓁 𝓁 𝓁 𝓁 𝓁 𝓁 𝓁

𝓁 𝓁 𝓁 𝓁 𝓁 𝓁 𝓁 𝓁 𝓁 𝓁 𝓁 𝓁 𝓁

𝓁 𝓁 𝓁 𝓁 𝓁 𝓁 𝓁 𝓁 𝓁 𝓁 𝓁 𝓁 𝓁

Now write the letter on your own.

𝓁

A B C D E F G H I J K L M N O P Q R S T U V W X Y Z

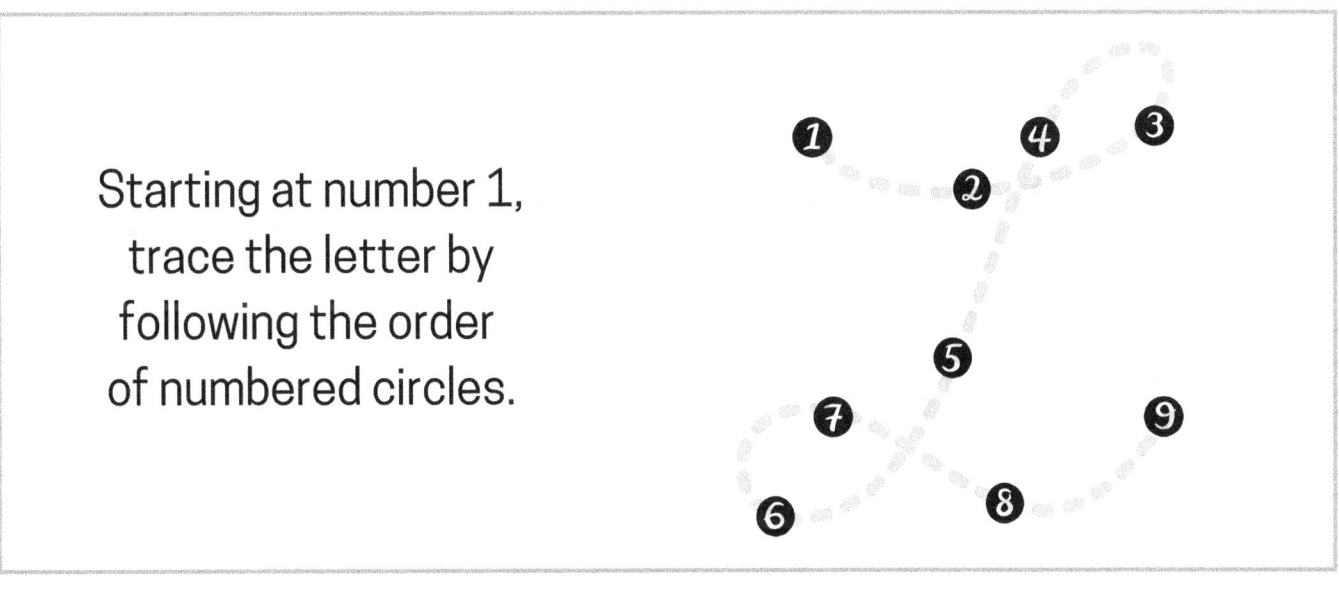

Starting at number 1, trace the letter by following the order of numbered circles.

Trace the letters using the example above.

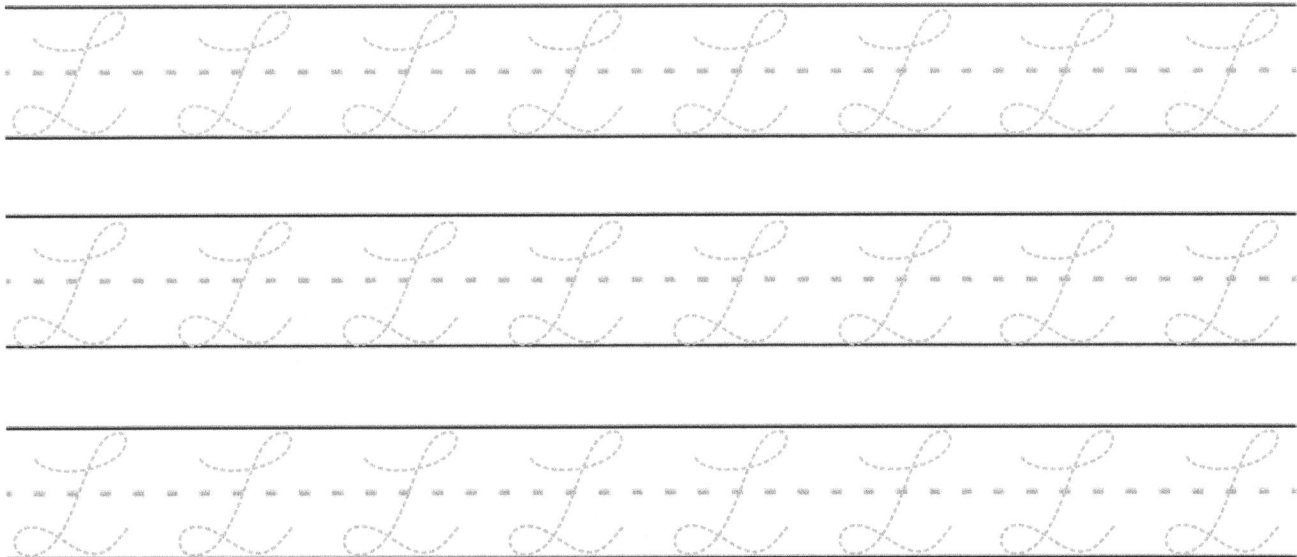

Now write the letter on your own.

L

a b c d e f g h i j k l **m** n o p q r s t u v w x y z

Starting at number 1, trace the letter by following the order of numbered circles.

Trace the letters using the example above.

m m m m m m m m

m m m m m m m m

m m m m m m m m

Now write the letter on your own.

m

A B C D E F G H I J K L **M** N O P Q R S T U V W X Y Z

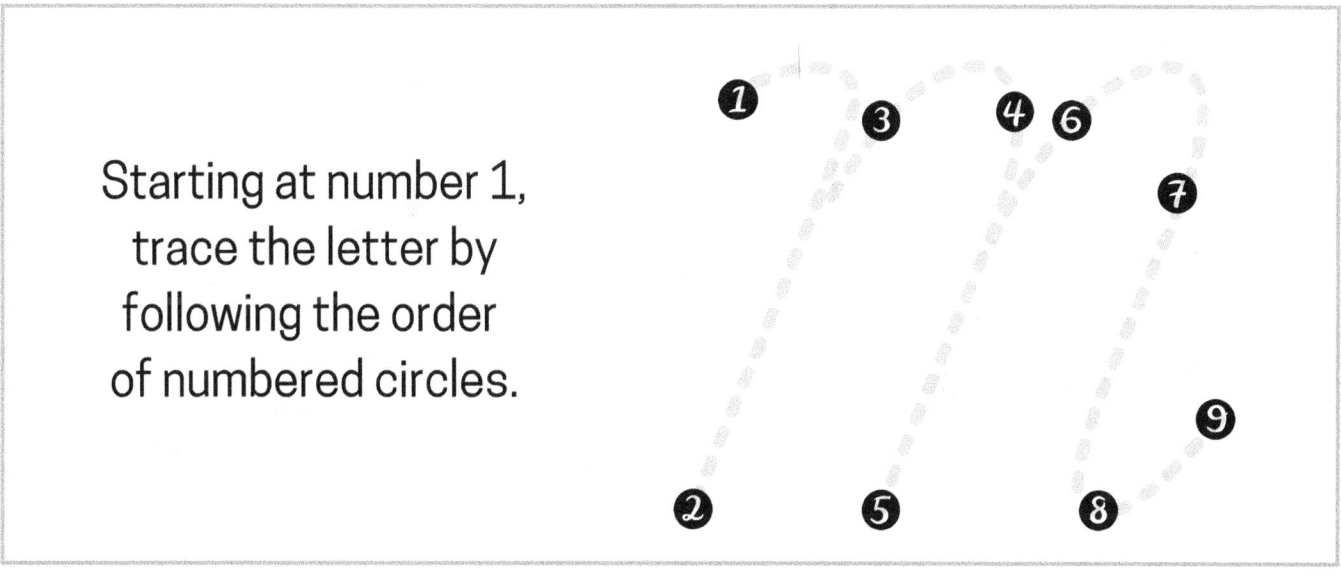

Starting at number 1, trace the letter by following the order of numbered circles.

Trace the letters using the example above.

Now write the letter on your own.

a b c d e f g h i j k l m **n** o p q r s t u v w x y z

Starting at number 1, trace the letter by following the order of numbered circles.

Trace the letters using the example above.

Now write the letter on your own.

A B C D E F G H I J K L M **n** O P Q R S T U V W X Y Z

Starting at number 1, trace the letter by following the order of numbered circles.

Trace the letters using the example above.

Now write the letter on your own.

a b c d e f g h i j k l m n **o** p q r s t u v w x y z

Starting at number 1, trace the letter by following the order of numbered circles.

Trace the letters using the example above.

Now write the letter on your own.

*A B C D E F G H I J K L M N **O** P Q R S T U V W X Y Z*

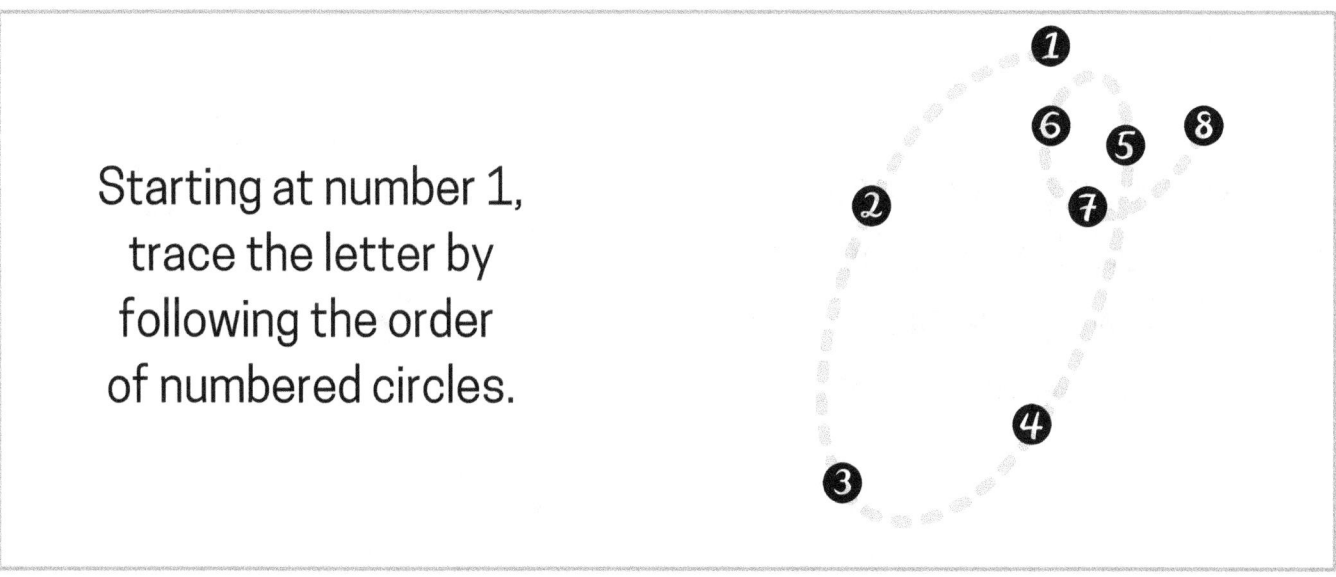

Starting at number 1, trace the letter by following the order of numbered circles.

Trace the letters using the example above.

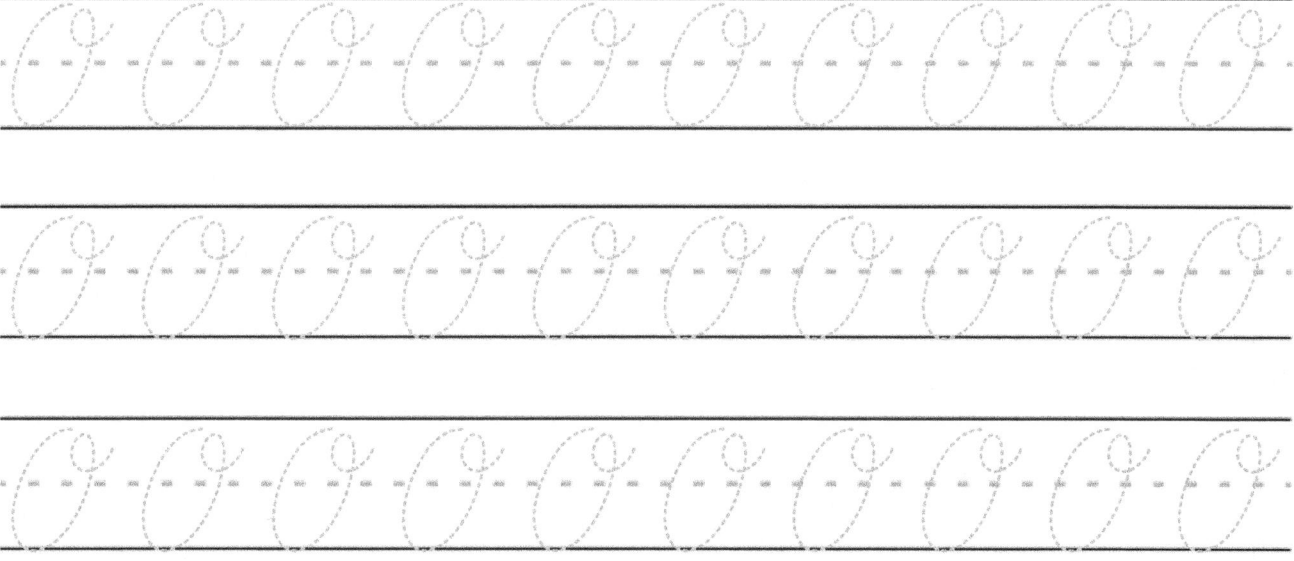

Now write the letter on your own.

O

a b c d e f g h i j k l m n o **p** q r s t u v w x y z

Starting at number 1, trace the letter by following the order of numbered circles.

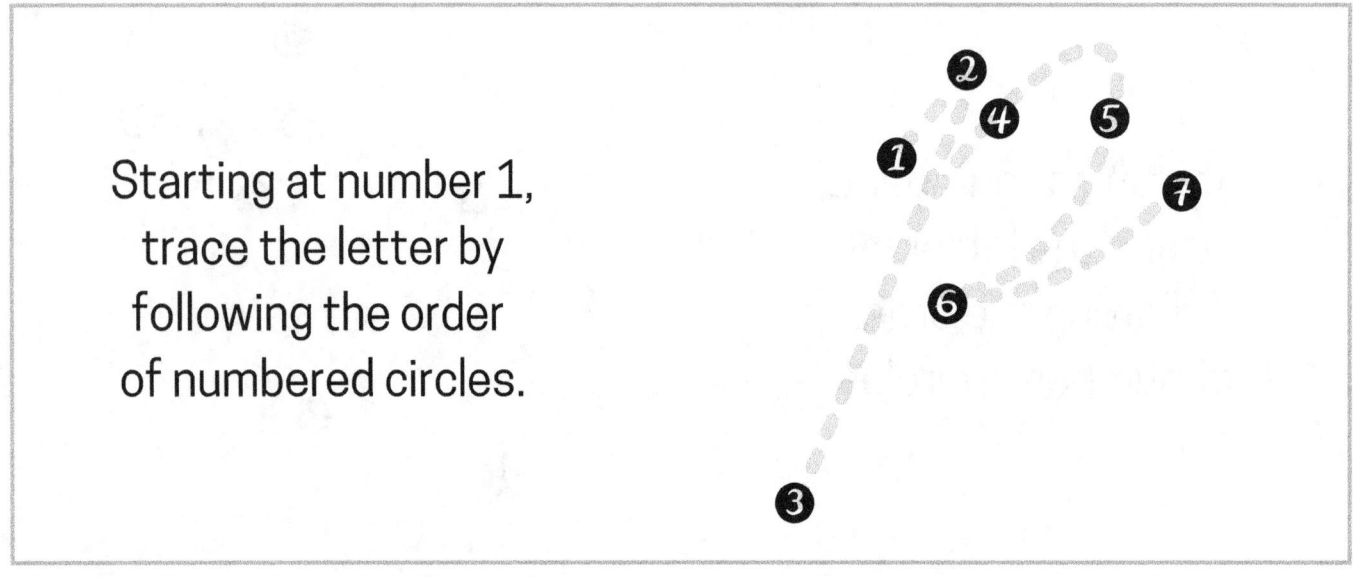

Trace the letters using the example above.

Now write the letter on your own.

𝑝

A B C D E F G H I J K L M N O **P** Q R S T U V W X Y Z

Starting at number 1, trace the letter by following the order of numbered circles.

Trace the letters using the example above.

Now write the letter on your own.

a b c d e f g h i j k l m n o p **q** *r s t u v w x y z*

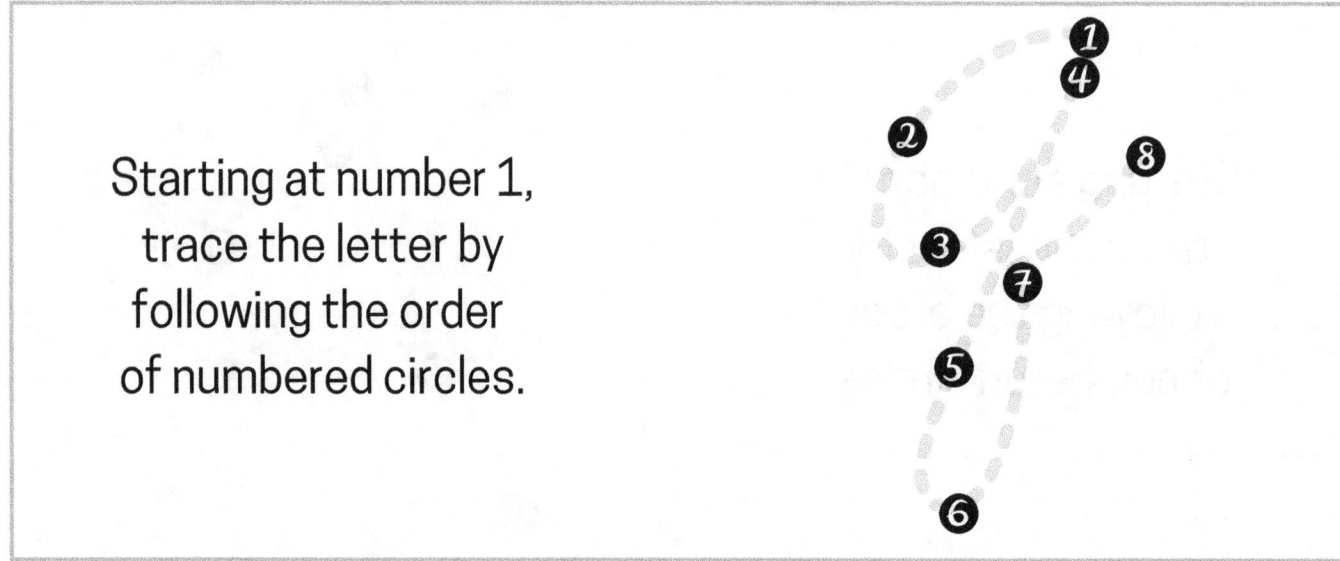

Starting at number 1, trace the letter by following the order of numbered circles.

Trace the letters using the example above.

Now write the letter on your own.

q

A B C D E F G H I J K L M N O P Q R S T U V W X Y Z

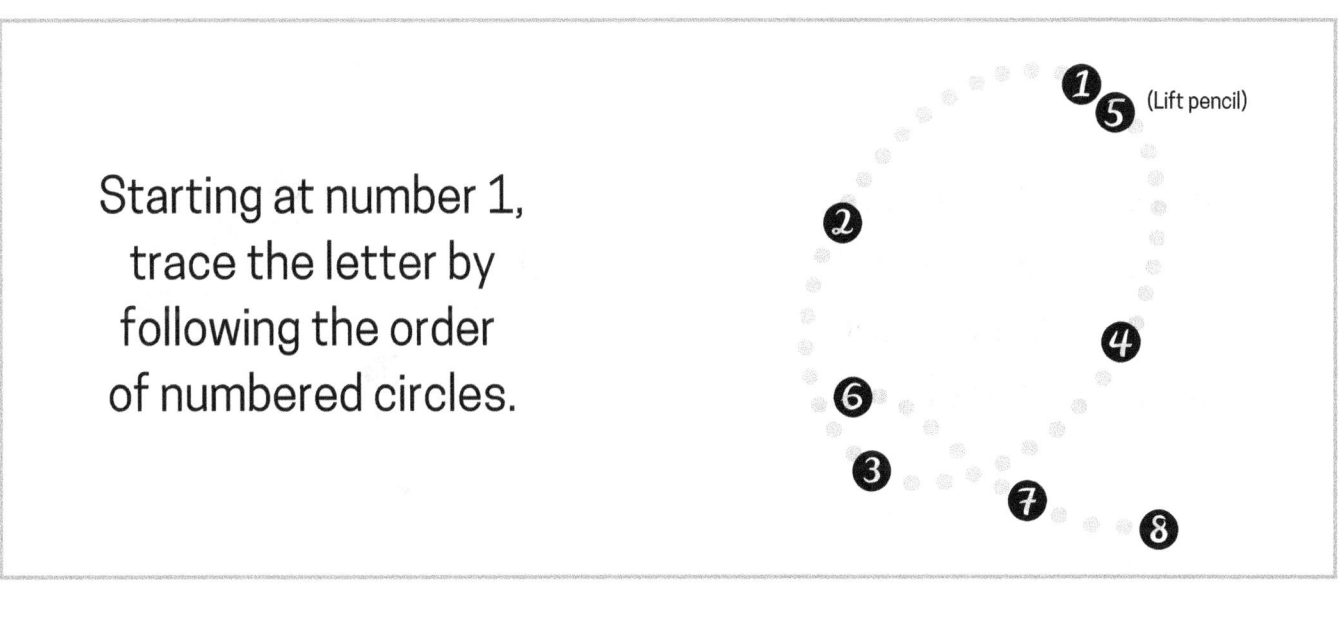

Starting at number 1, trace the letter by following the order of numbered circles.

Trace the letters using the example above.

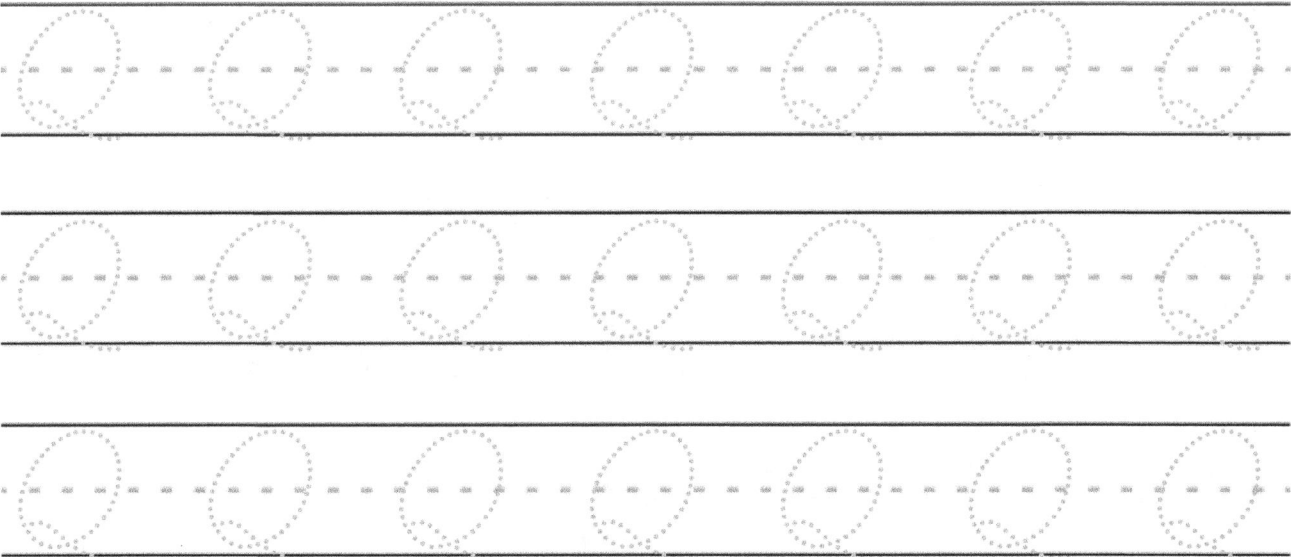

Now write the letter on your own.

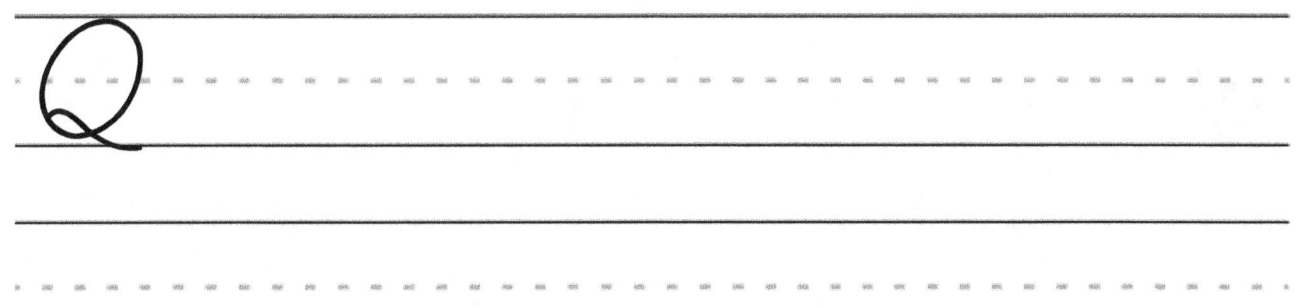

a b c d e f g h i j k l m n o p q **r** *s t u v w x y z*

Starting at number 1, trace the letter by following the order of numbered circles.

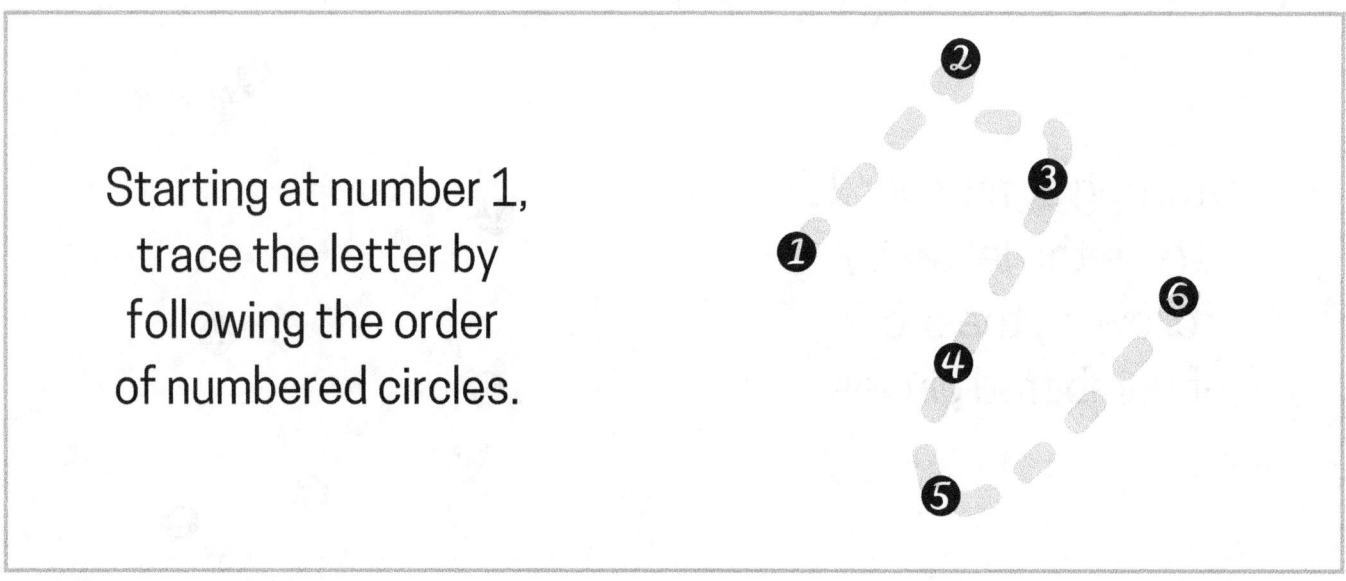

Trace the letters using the example above.

Now write the letter on your own.

A B C D E F G H I J K L M N O P Q **R** *S T U V W X Y Z*

Starting at number 1, trace the letter by following the order of numbered circles.

Trace the letters using the example above.

Now write the letter on your own.

R

a b c d e f g h i j k l m n o p q r **s** t u v w x y z

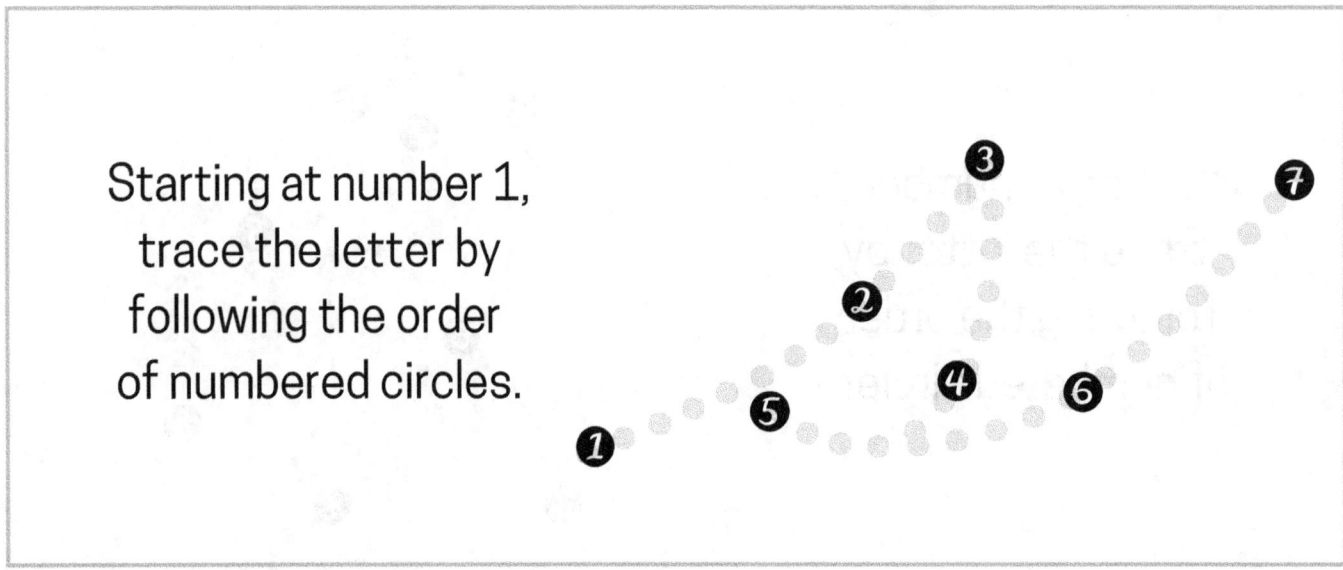

Starting at number 1, trace the letter by following the order of numbered circles.

Trace the letters using the example above.

Now write the letter on your own.

A B C D E F G H I J K L M N O P Q R **S** *T U V W X Y Z*

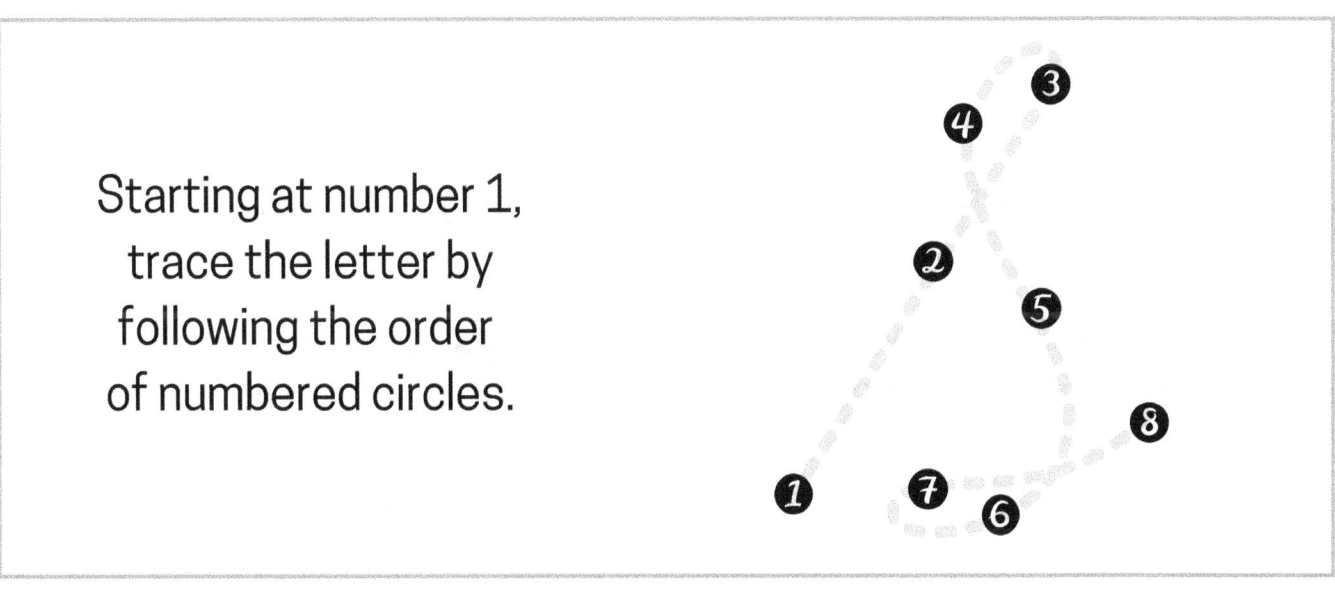

Starting at number 1, trace the letter by following the order of numbered circles.

Trace the letters using the example above.

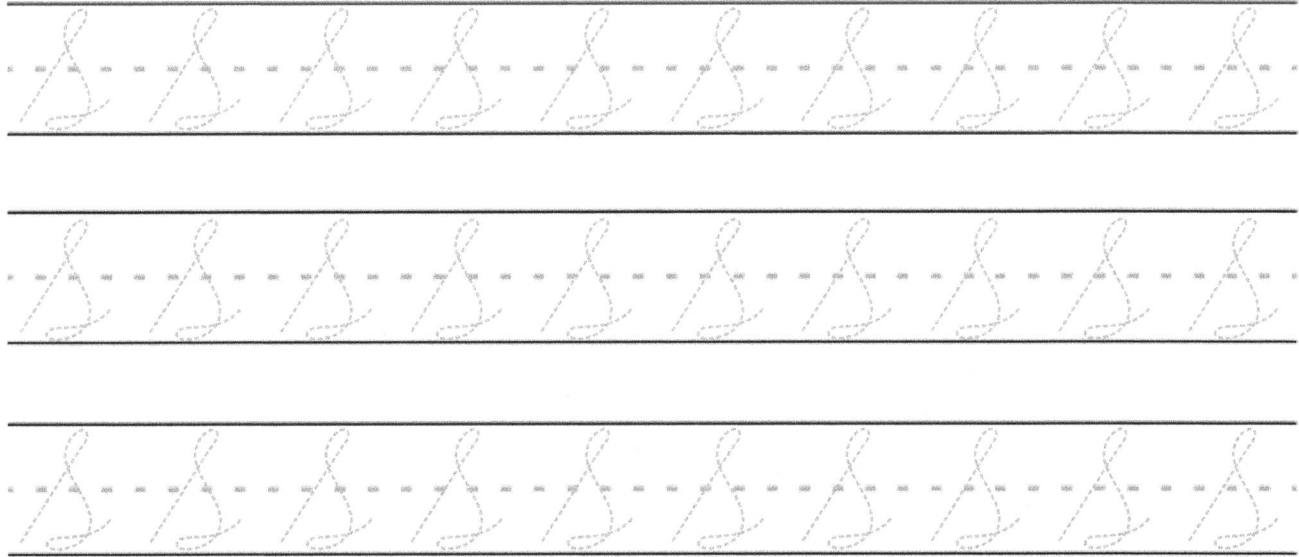

Now write the letter on your own.

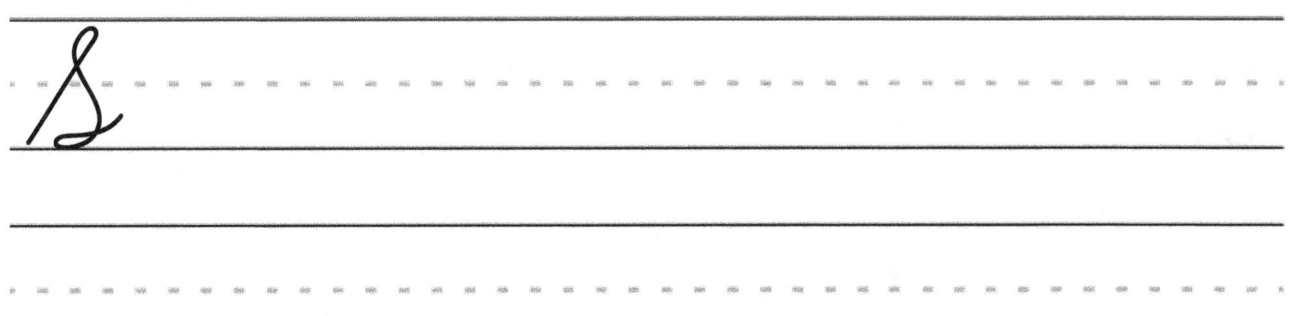

a b c d e f g h i j k l m n o p q r s **t** *u v w x y z*

Starting at number 1, trace the letter by following the order of numbered circles.

(Lift pencil)

Trace the letters using the example above.

t t t t t t t t t t

t t t t t t t t t t

t t t t t t t t t t

Now write the letter on your own.

t

A B C D E F G H I J K L M N O P Q R S T U V W X Y Z

Starting at number 1, trace the letter by following the order of numbered circles.

❶ ❸ ❷ (Lift pencil)

❹

Trace the letters using the example above.

Now write the letter on your own.

a b c d e f g h i j k l m n o p q r s t **u** v w x y z

Starting at number 1, trace the letter by following the order of numbered circles.

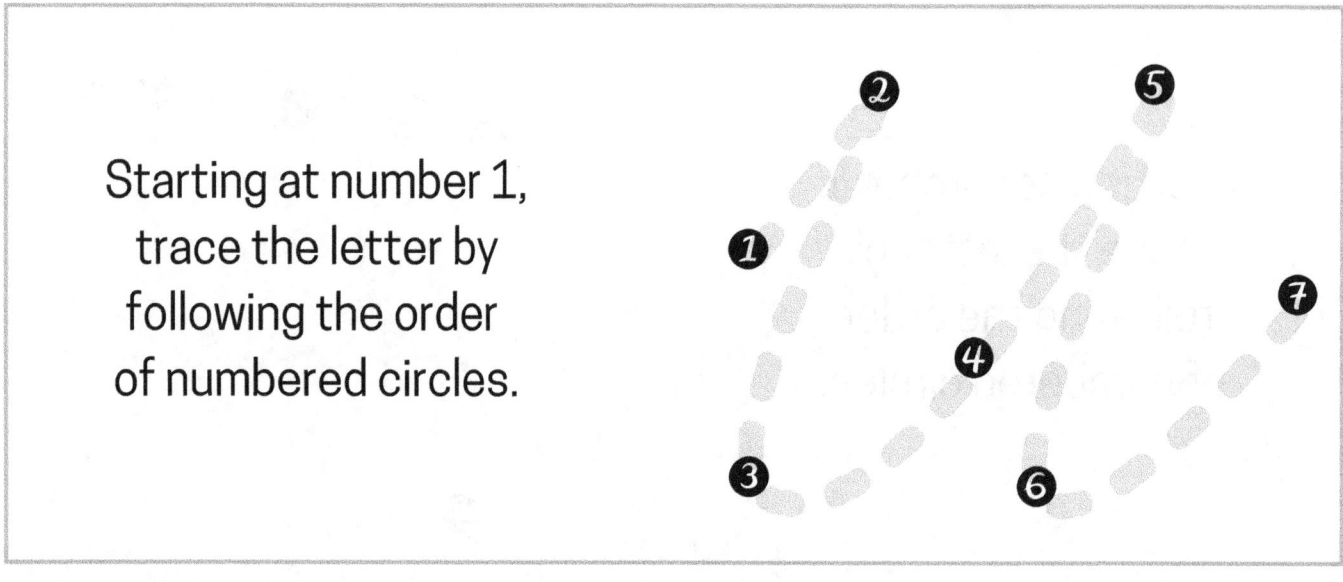

Trace the letters using the example above.

Now write the letter on your own.

*A B C D E F G H I J K L M N O P Q R S T **U** V W X Y Z*

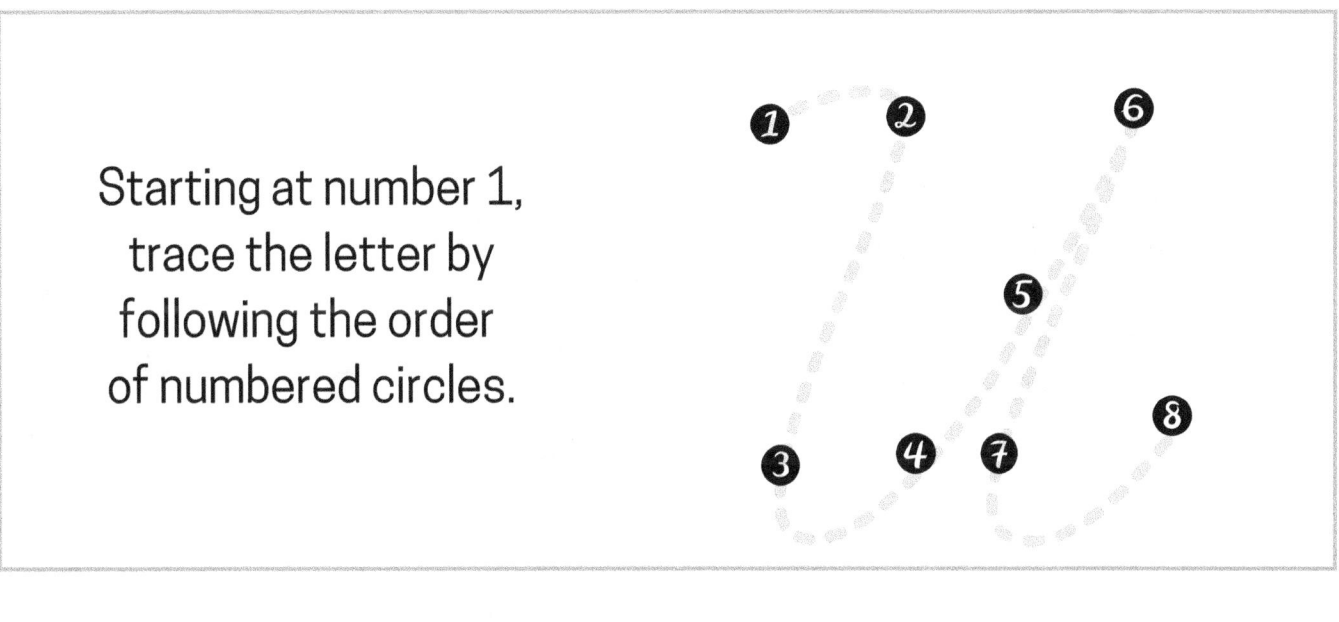

Starting at number 1, trace the letter by following the order of numbered circles.

Trace the letters using the example above.

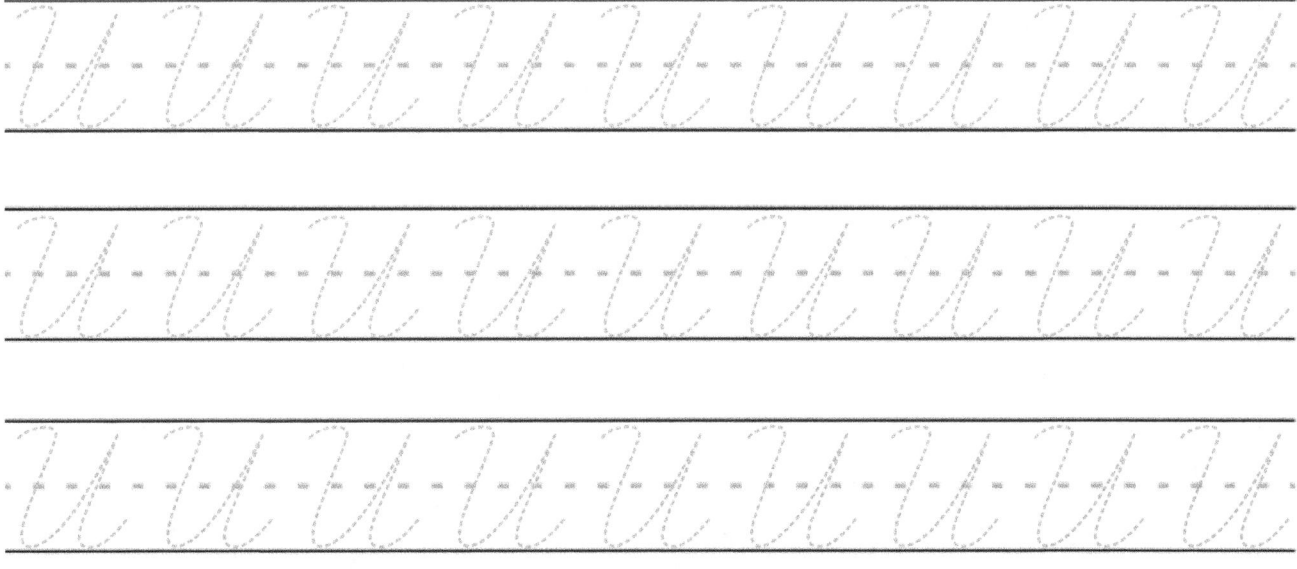

Now write the letter on your own.

𝓊

a b c d e f g h i j k l m n o p q r s t u **u** w x y z

Starting at number 1, trace the letter by following the order of numbered circles.

Trace the letters using the example above.

Now write the letter on your own.

u

*A B C D E F G H I J K L M N O P Q R S T U **V** W X Y Z*

Starting at number 1, trace the letter by following the order of numbered circles.

Trace the letters using the example above.

Now write the letter on your own.

a b c d e f g h i j k l m n o p q r s t u v **w** x y z

Starting at number 1, trace the letter by following the order of numbered circles.

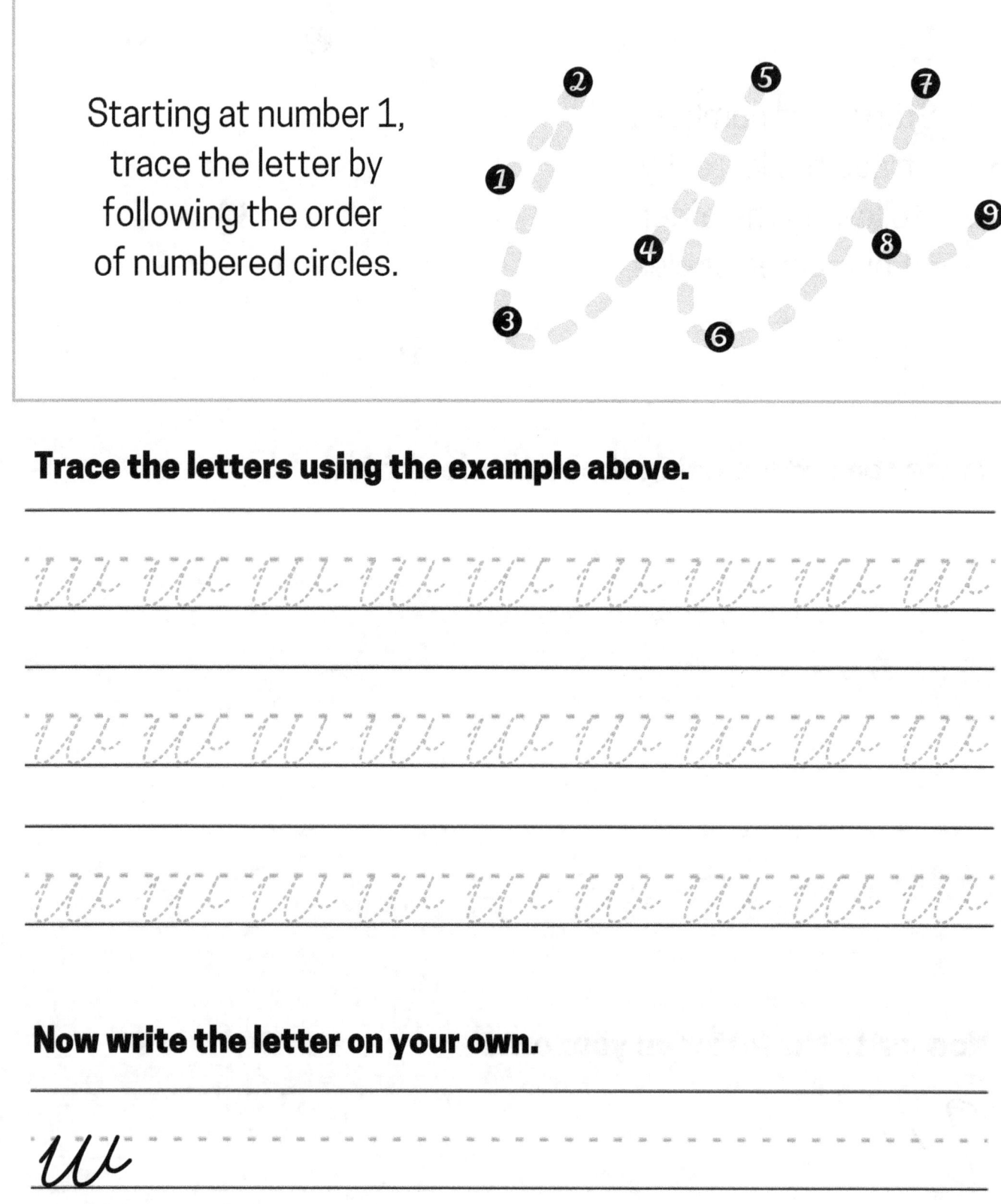

Trace the letters using the example above.

Now write the letter on your own.

*A B C D E F G H I J K L M N O P Q R S T U V **W** X Y Z*

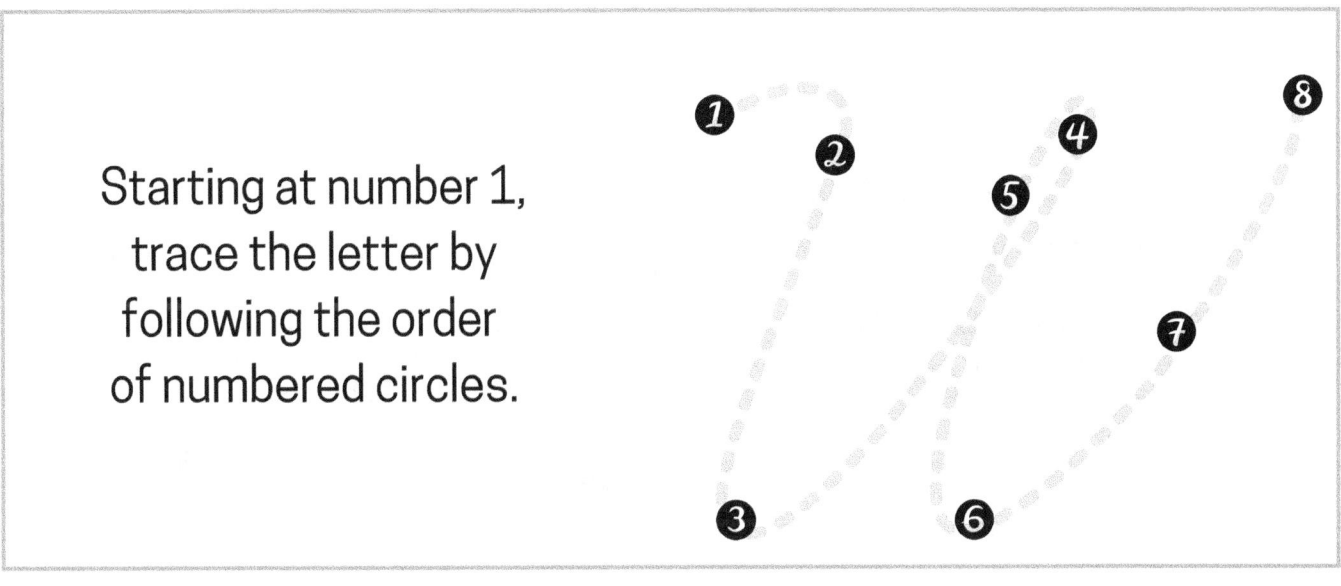

Starting at number 1, trace the letter by following the order of numbered circles.

Trace the letters using the example above.

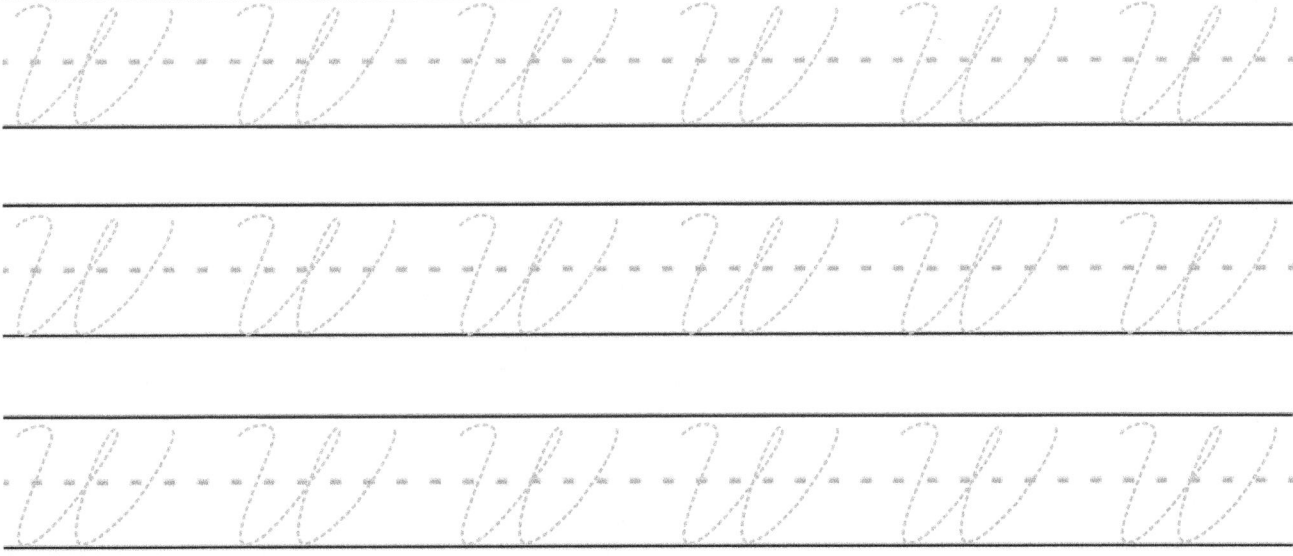

Now write the letter on your own.

𝓌

a b c d e f g h i j k l m n o p q r s t u v w **x** *y z*

Starting at number 1, trace the letter by following the order of numbered circles.

(Lift pencil)

Trace the letters using the example above.

Now write the letter on your own.

x

A B C D E F G H I J K L M N O P Q R S T U V W **X** *Y Z*

Starting at number 1, trace the letter by following the order of numbered circles.

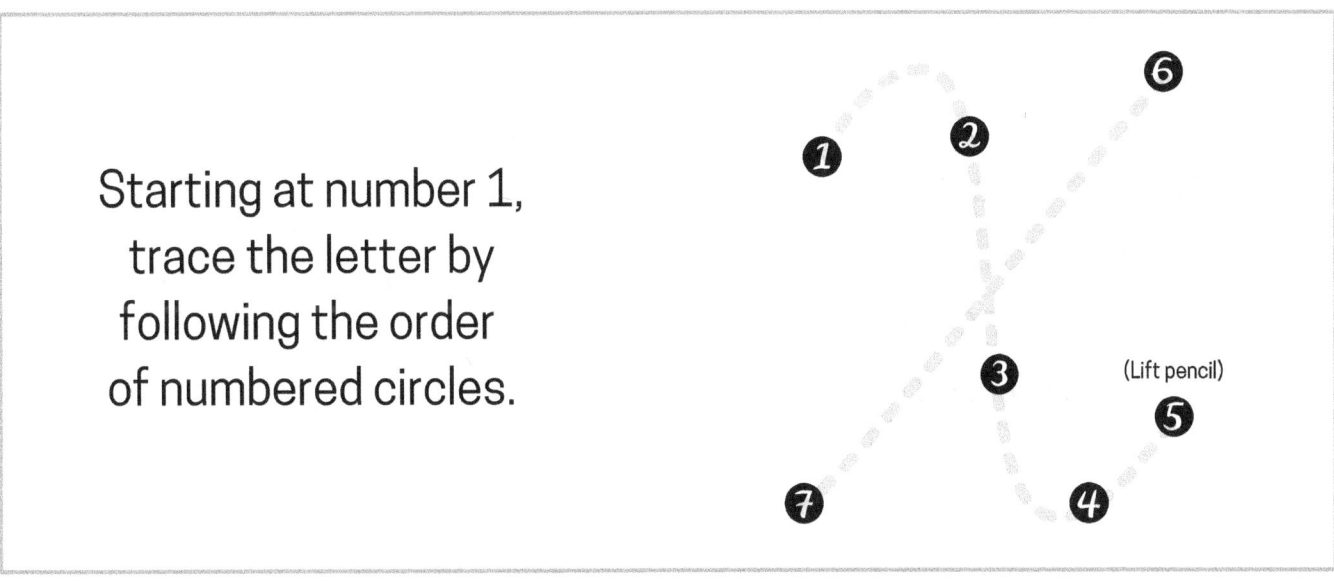

(Lift pencil)

Trace the letters using the example above.

Now write the letter on your own.

a b c d e f g h i j k l m n o p q r s t u v w x **y** z

Starting at number 1, trace the letter by following the order of numbered circles.

Trace the letters using the example above.

Now write the letter on your own.

y

A B C D E F G H I J K L M N O P Q R S T U V W X  Z

Starting at number 1, trace the letter by following the order of numbered circles.

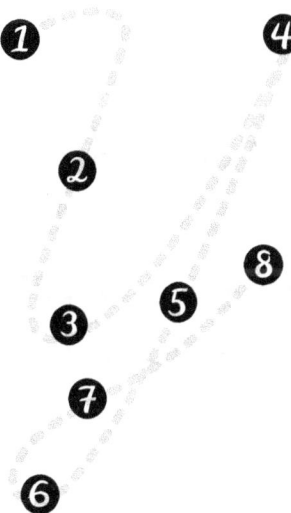

Trace the letters using the example above.

Now write the letter on your own.

a b c d e f g h i j k l m n o p q r s t u v w x y **z**

Starting at number 1, trace the letter by following the order of numbered circles.

Trace the letters using the example above.

Now write the letter on your own.

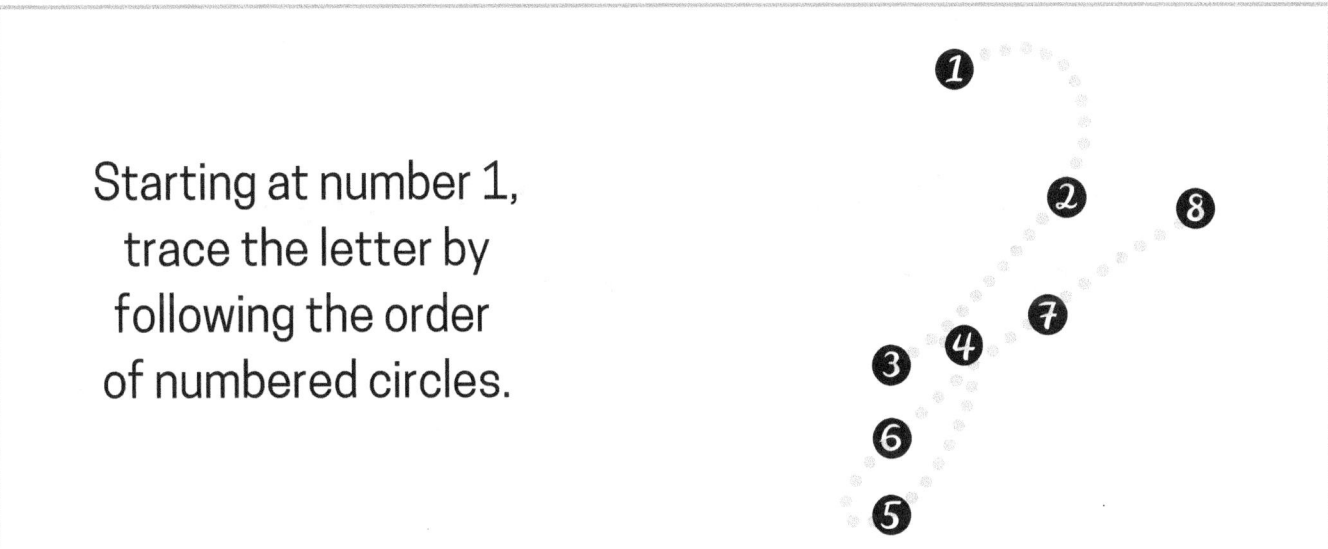

Trace the letters using the example above.

Now write the letter on your own.

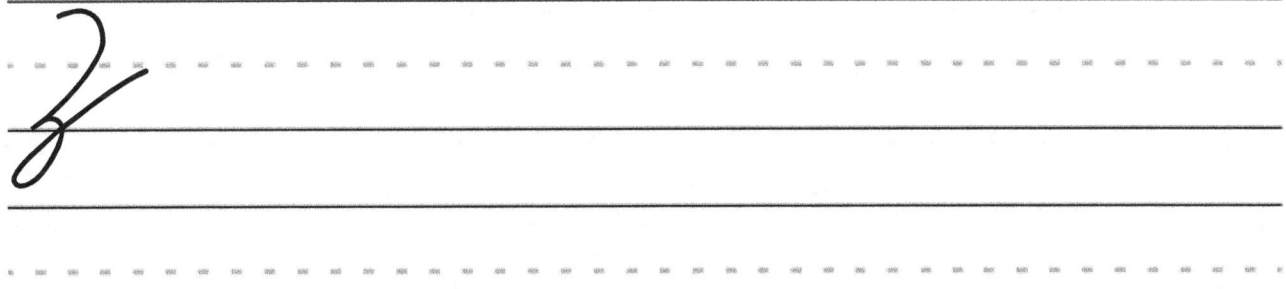

a b c d e f g h i j k l m n o p q r s t u v w x y z

A B C D E F G H I J K L M N O P Q R S T U V W X Y Z

Use this blank page to practice any letters that you found difficult.

Connecting Letters

In this part we learn to join two letters together. Follow the numbers to trace both letters and learn how they are linked.

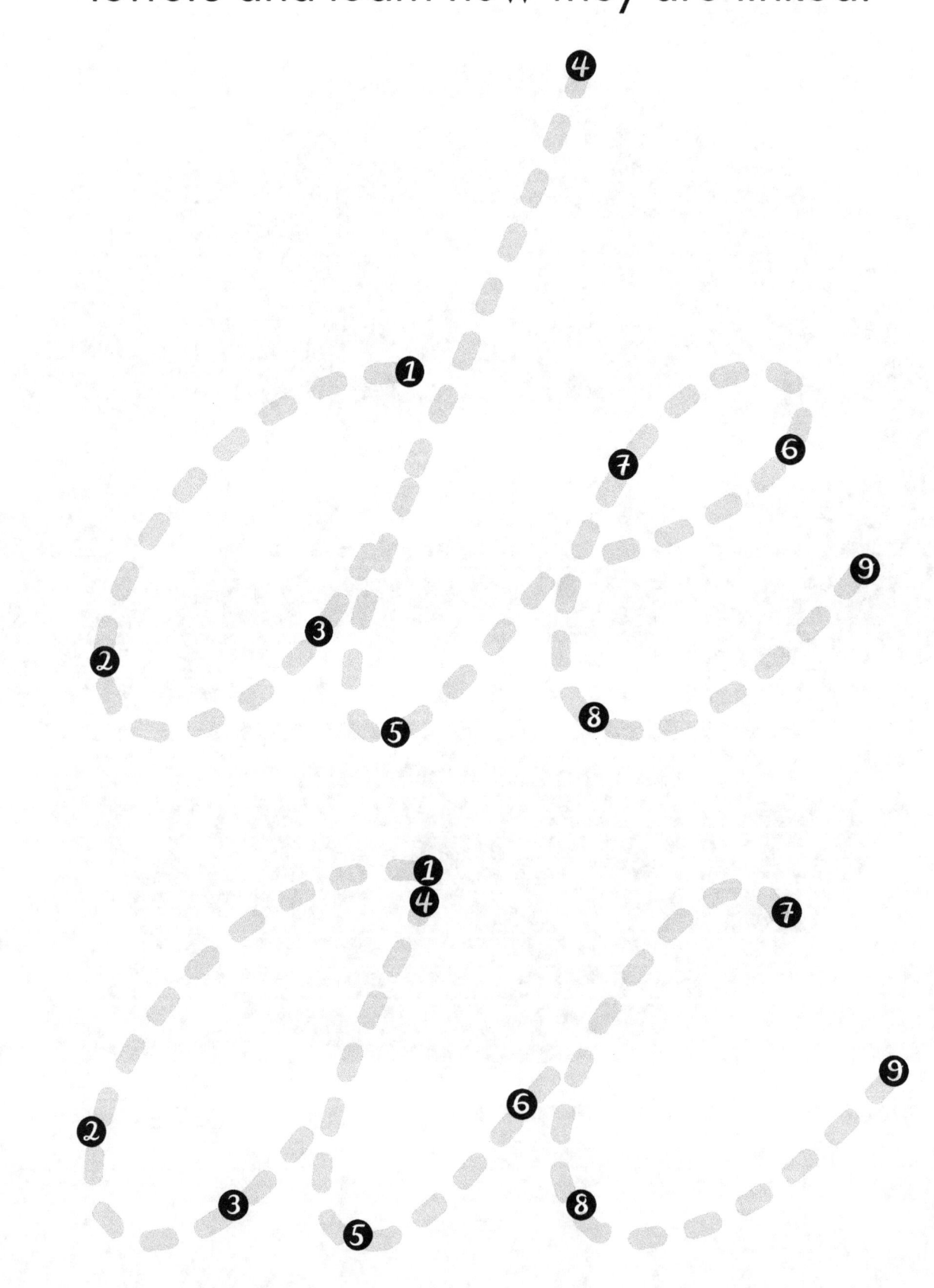

Let's go over a few more examples of linking letters.

(Lift pencil)

Trace the connected letters and then write them on your own

ge ge ge ge ge ge ge ge

ge

tl tl tl tl tl tl tl tl

tl

uu uu uu uu uu

uu

Trace the connected letters and then write them on your own

yc yc yc yc yc yc yc

yc

ju ju ju ju ju ju ju

ju

cc cc cc cc cc cc cc cc

cc

Trace the connected letters and then write them on your own

ma ma ma ma ma

ma

dp dp dp dp dp dp

dp

bi bi bi bi bi bi bi

bi

Trace the connected letters and then write them on your own

gg gg gg gg gg gg gg

gg

fk fk fk fk fk fk fk

fk

hn hn hn hn hn hn

hn

Trace the connected letters and then write them on your own

qr qr qr qr qr qr qr

qr

xy xy xy xy xy xy

xy

tu tu tu tu tu tu tu

tu

Trace the connected letters and then write them on your own

He He He He He He

He

Ja Ja Ja Ja Ja Ja

Ja

Kc Kc Kc Kc Kc Kc

Kc

Trace the connected letters and then write them on your own

Lp Lp Lp Lp Lp

Lp

Yb Yb Yb Yb Yb Yb

Yb

Cc Cc Cc Cc Cc Cc Cc

Cc

Part 2: Writing Words

baby baby baby baby

Trace the dotted word and then write it in the remaining lines beneath.

girl girl girl girl girl

lunch   lunch   lunch

Trace the dotted word and then write it in the remaining lines beneath.

away   away   away

nice nice nice nice

Trace the dotted word and then write it in the remaining lines beneath.

candy candy candy

drive drive drive

Trace the dotted word and then write it in the remaining lines beneath.

very very very very

club club club club

Trace the dotted word and then write it in the remaining lines beneath.

what what what

farm   farm   farm

**Trace the dotted word and then write
it in the remaining lines beneath.**

riding   riding   riding

each each each each

Trace the dotted word and then write it in the remaining lines beneath.

tree tree tree tree tree

heard heard heard

Trace the dotted word and then write it in the remaining lines beneath.

family family family

cattle cattle cattle

Trace the dotted word and then write it in the remaining lines beneath.

dinner dinner dinner

Kitten Kitten Kitten

Trace the dotted word and then write it in the remaining lines beneath.

Large Large Large

inches   inches   inches

Trace the dotted word and then write it in the remaining lines beneath.

Juice   Juice   Juice

Shield Shield Shield

Trace the dotted word and then write it in the remaining lines beneath.

Running Running

Merry Merry Merry

Trace the dotted word and then write it in the remaining lines beneath.

Picture Picture Picture

Winter Winter Winter

Trace the dotted word and then write it in the remaining lines beneath.

Xray Xray Xray

Under Under Under

Trace the dotted word and then write it in the remaining lines beneath.

Value Value Value

remember remember

Trace the dotted word and then write it in the remaining lines beneath.

yesterday yesterday

President   President

Trace the dotted word and then write it in the remaining lines beneath.

Sentence   Sentence

Different   Different

Trace the dotted word and then write it in the remaining lines beneath.

Suddenly   Suddenly

medicine   medicine

Trace the dotted word and then write it in the remaining lines beneath.

maximum   maximum

happiness happiness

Trace the dotted word and then write
it in the remaining lines beneath.

Beautiful Beautiful

I am great at writing

Trace the dotted word and then write it in the remaining lines beneath.

Let's try sentences

Part 3: Writing Sentences

I will stand next to my best friend at the back of the hall.

The water in the pond is ten feet below the trees.

We all stood around the teacher on the first day of school.

She read the scary story under the covers with a light.

Should we knock on my brother's door to see how he is?

An atom is a small particle you cannot see with your eyes.

Watch the massive cloud change direction in the clear sky.

My teacher showed me how to solve the math problem.

We can get closer to the huge giraffe in the exotic zoo.

The noise from the fountain began to grow much louder.

My mother read a book by an author who taught writing.

We were almost at the top of the stairs when he tripped.

Compare the triangle and the sqaure on the poster of shapes.

The telescope is used to magnify planets in the dark night sky.

She put a yellow flower in her hair as she went out.

We will visit the farmers market in the week after next.

My mom works in the garden every day until it gets dark.

Strong crops give them an advantage in the long winter.

The explorer had to swim under the branches in the lake.

You should always brush your teeth before you go to bed.

The dog buried his bone while the cat sniffed around him

www.ingramcontent.com/pod-product-compliance
Lightning Source LLC
Chambersburg PA
CBHW081352080526
44588CB00016B/2474